JOY OF THE ROVERS

JOY OF THE
ROVERS!

JACK STEGGLES

MAINSTREAM
PUBLISHING

First published in Great Britain in 1990 by
MAINSTREAM PUBLISHING COMPANY (EDINBURGH) LTD
7 Albany Street
Edinburgh EH1 3UG

British Library Cataloguing in Publication Data
Steggles, Jack
    Joy of the Rovers!
    1. England. Association Football. Clubs. Bristol Rovers
    Football Club, history
    I. Title
796.334630942393

ISBN 1-85158-347-5

Pictures courtesy of Bristol Rovers F.C.

Typeset in Imprint by Bookworm Typesetting, Edinburgh.
Printed in Great Britain by Billings & Sons, Worcester.

This book is dedicated to
Bristol Rovers fans everywhere.

Contents

Foreword

HARD-NOSED cynics who claim there is no romance left in big-time professional football have had their theory exploded by the incredible exploits of Bristol Rovers. For the unfashionable, hard-up club from the West Country have provided one of the greatest success stories of all time – triumphing against overwhelming odds to win the Third Division Championship. Manager Gerry Francis has earned the title of "Miracle Worker" for what he has achieved with the Rovers bunch of soccer nomads – a team put together for next-to-nothing and without a ground or training ground to call their own. Home matches are played on the Twerton Park ground of Bath City, 12 miles down the M4.

"Pirates", "Black Arabs" and "Gasheads" are among the nick-names Rovers have had since they were formed 107 years ago. Francis coined a new one for them when he took over as manager of the ailing, debt-ridden club three years ago – "Ragbag Rovers".

"That was the only way to describe them. I could not believe what I had walked into, for they had absolutely nothing," recalls Francis – who locals believe should have been knighted in the Queen's Birthday Honours list for what he has achieved there. "I have been pretty successful in business, with three limited companies outside football. So one of the things I have learned to do is read a balance sheet. And when I looked at Rovers' one before taking the job I did not think they would last a year.

"Things were so bad I honestly thought they would go

out of business. The bookies down here did not give us much hope either, for they made us 2-1 favourites for relegation to the Fourth Division. I responded to that by telling the players: 'Stick with me and I will get you 3-1.' But we have managed to prove them wrong with a lot of hard work and tough economic measures."

Francis even delivered the goods, steering Rovers to their first promotion since 1974, when they finished runners-up to Oldham in the Third Division, despite having to sell his two best players – Gary Penrice and Nigel Martyn.

The bottom dropped out of the world of already demoralised supporters when Penrice, the leading scorer for the previous two years and a hero with the fans, went to Watford for £500,000 and Martyn became Britain's first million-pound goalkeeper with a move to Crystal Palace. Even some of the team feared the worst after those two were sold within days of each other back in November. But they had to go, for when you were in the sort of financial mess the Rovers were, offers like that are simply too good to turn down.

But Francis soon put the sparkle back in the eye and the bounce back in the step of his players, who went on to produce a fairy tale. What Rovers managed to do in the face of overwhelming odds is *Roy of the Rovers* stuff – even some Sunday morning pub teams have better facilities than they do!

They train on the sports ground of a chocolate factory on the outskirts of Bristol. Everything they own is kept locked in rickety Portakabins at that ground and is moved lock, stock and barrel to Bath for matches – and back again afterwards.

The country's pampered, overpaid glamour-club stars would run a mile if confronted with a situation like this. Rovers' bunch of down-to-earth players got on with it – and overcame it superbly. The 13 men who won the championship for Rovers, and took them to Wembley to face Tranmere Rovers in the final of the Leyland-Daf Cup, were put together for peanuts. Eleven of them were free transfers. Players given away by other clubs who had no further use for them. The other two cost the princely sum of £80,000 – and most of that went on one player.

After losing Penrice to Watford and Tony Sealy with injury, Francis managed to persuade the Rovers Board to give him £70,000 to buy Carl Saunders from Stoke City. Saunders was a no more than average full-back, languishing in the reserves at Stoke. But Francis saw something in him other managers did not, converted him to a front player and Carl started scoring as soon as he went into the Rovers team.

The other £10,000 went on Ian Holloway. Francis was so keen

Gary Penrice, sold for £500,000 to Watford, in action against Cardiff.

to get the former Rovers player back he loaned the desperately hard-up club the money to buy him out of his own pocket! Shrewd businessman Francis got a handsome dividend on his investment. For Holloway regained the form the manager knew he was capable of and played a significant part in Rovers' unforgettable season.

It was also Gerry's way of giving something back to Rovers' loyal fans. For when he first joined the Rovers as a player they clubbed together to pay his wages each week. That proves the spirit that exists at this lovely little club. Rovers have been in deep, deep trouble and everyone who cares about them has pulled together to help them out of it. They are back in the Second Division for the first time since 1981 and the future at last looks safe for a club who have been one of the game's poor relations ever since they were formed in 1893.

They started as the Black Arabs and a year later changed to Eastville Rovers. That became Bristol Eastville Rovers when they moved to that ground in 1897, and 12 months later the "Eastville" was dropped to give them their present name.

In 70 years as a League club they have never even threatened to disturb the peace of the game's élite and the highest placing

Mascots enjoying their big day.

they have ever managed was sixth in the Second Division, twice back in the 1950s. They have twice reached the quarter-finals of the FA Cup and League Cup, now the Rumbelows League Cup. And they earned a permanent place in the record books — for the wrong reasons — in 1936. That's when they suffered their heaviest-ever defeat, an astonishing 12-0 at Luton. Ten of the goals were scored by Hatters' striker Joe Payne — a feat that has never been equalled and that earned the player the privilege of having a lounge named after him at Luton's Kenilworth Road ground.

Rovers may never have been one of football's most glamorous or successful clubs, but they have always been one of the friendliest, breeding a fierce sense of pride and loyalty in everyone connected with them.

Jack Pitt is a prime example. He joined the club in 1946 and was a member of the team that won promotion from the Third Division in 1952/3. It was the first time Rovers had ever left the Third Division and, like the current team, they finished as proud champions. Pitt is still with the club and celebrated his 70th birthday the day Rovers met Tranmere in the Leyland-Daf final at Wembley. What a pity Rovers, beaten 2-1 in controversial circumstances, could not have become the first team to complete the Third and Fourth Division "double" and given long-serving Jack the finest birthday

Rovers fans in celebratory mood.

present he could have asked for.

Geoff Bradford, Harry Bamford, George Petherbridge and Ray Mabbutt are others to give years of sterling service to Rovers. Mabbutt, of course, is the father of footballing sons Gary and Kevin. Gary – who was transferred to Tottenham for a giveaway £105,000 and has since earned full England honours – is probably the most famous player ever produced by the club. Kevin was an outstanding talent, whose career was cut short by injury. For reasons best known to himself he decided to play for hated rivals Bristol City – a subject taboo in these pages. Gary, who has overcome diabetes to get to the top of his demanding, physically tough profession, still follows Rovers' fortunes closely and was as thrilled as anyone at what they achieved last season.

Stuart Taylor was another to give the club years of outstanding service. He holds the appearance record, with 545 League games between 1966 and 1980.

It is claimed that players never actually "leave" Rovers. They just move away and play for someone else, with part of them always remaining in Bristol. And the close-knit feeling they engender in the club was explained by chairman Denis Dunford after Rovers – the section's outstanding team – failed to get one player in the Third Division representative side chosen by fellow professionals and announced at the PFA Awards Dinner towards the end of the season.

"That does not surprise or disappoint me in the slightest. Here at Rovers we are a team – so how can you single out individuals from such a strong unit?" said Dunford.

That sums up the philosophy at Rovers, a club where everyone closed ranks and stood shoulder to shoulder to fight for their very existence. They have come through the dark days and now the sun is beginning to shine on them. Only the hard-hearted would begrudge them that after all they have been through.

Rovers hope to have a new ground in Mangotsfield in around three years' time. At the moment that's all they have . . . hope. But that is a lot more than they have had in recent years. In the meantime they will soldier on as part-time tenants at non-League Bath.

They are no longer the poor relations, football's scavengers. The pride is back in place; they are making money at last and it has all turned out joy for the Rovers.

1

Gerry Francis

Manager

F RIDAY, 15 JUNE 1990 was a very happy day for all Bristol
Rovers supporters. It was the day highly valued manager
Gerry Francis signed a new one-year contract with the club
to end all speculation about his immediate future.

It was an act that was to keep Gerry at the club to lead them into
the Second Division. And one that frustrated Aston Villa's dramatic
approach for him. Villa wanted Gerry to take over from Graham
Taylor, who had moved up to take charge of England. But their
approach for him was turned down flat by the Rovers Board, who
refused rival chairman Doug Ellis permission to speak to him. So
Villa got no further than West Ham, Portsmouth and Swindon –
who had all placed the name of Gerry Francis high on their wanted
list.

"Aston Villa are a big club and any manager with ambition
would fancy being their manager. So it was obviously a
disappointment when I never got the chance to talk to
them," says Francis. "When the Rovers Board refused
Doug Ellis permission to approach me I could have walked
out. But it would have been the height of hypocrisy to do
that.

"I have always preached honesty and integrity to my
players and could not have lived with myself if I had not
shown those same qualities at this time. I have stressed
that if you sign a contract – or even shake hands on
a verbal agreement – you should honour it. And that's

precisely what I knew I had to do when Villa showed an interest.

"I had signed that one-year contract just a month earlier and will now be at Bristol Rovers until at least the end of next season. I only ever sign one-year contracts so that I can be in a position to control my own destiny. I have never believed in so-called long-term security, or tying myself to one place for too long."

Rovers fans have lived with the dread of losing Gerry for the past couple of years. His superb management has brought the good times back to the homely little West Country club and what he has achieved against crippling odds has been fantastic.

His efforts have not gone unnoticed higher up the ladder and the 37-year-old Francis is now one of the most wanted young managers in the business. Swindon wanted him last summer, after Lou Macari left them to embark on his ill-fated spell as manager of West Ham.

"Brian Hillier, their chairman at the time, contacted me to ask if I wanted the job. He was quite entitled to come direct to me because I was out of contract at Rovers," says Francis. "But I had agreed verbally to sign a new one and shaken hands on it with Rovers' chairman Denis Dunford. So I told Brian to contact the club and said we would take it from there. That's the last I heard of it."

That was a relief to Rovers' adoring fans, who had gone to astonishing lengths to keep their man at the club. A campaign was launched that Gerry later admitted he found absolutely overwhelming. A staggering 5,000 postcards were sent to his Surrey home. The cards depicted a cartoon character and bore the slogan "Please don't go Gerry". Francis has kept all those cards. He cherishes every one of them and says: "You would have to be pretty thick-skinned to ignore a gesture like that." But as much as those fans want their idol to stay, they accept the harsh reality that they cannot hold on to him forever and know that a move to bigger and better things is inevitable.

They feared the worst during the summer after Gerry led the team he put together for next-to-nothing to the Third Division championship and the Leyland-Daf Cup final against Tranmere Rovers at Wembley. But after thinking long and hard for several weeks Gerry knew he still had a job to do with Rovers and decided to give at least one more year to settle them in the Second Division.

So on that sunny Friday morning of 15 June, Gerry left his Bagshot home, pointed his car towards the M4 and drove down to Bristol to

Gerry Francis.

attend a packed Press conference and sign a new contract.

The man did not have to do it. In fact he has no need to stay in management at all – a profession he calls hazardous and stressful. He is a highly successful businessman outside the game, with three limited companies and a bank balance that will make him secure for the rest of his life. So why do it? Why stay with a club used to living from hand to mouth and for years among football's poor relations?

"We started a job together and it is not finished yet. There is only so far any manager can go with a club – but I have not reached that point yet. Besides, I owe the West Country people something," says Francis.

"We have already talked about the reactions when I had the chance to leave last summer. What the fans did in sending all those cards made it clear how much they wanted to keep me here. And when I came to the club in 1985 as a player those same fans clubbed together to help pay my wages, because the club could not afford to do it. There would be something wrong if you conveniently forgot things like that."

Francis has paid his dues to Rovers with the success he has brought them and could walk out now owing them nothing. And the club was lucky to get him, for his first taste of management left such a bitter taste in his mouth he vowed he would never give it another go. That was at Exeter in 1983. He went in thinking he had nothing to worry about, got the shock of his life . . . and was sacked after just nine months.

"That bitter experience taught me that no matter what you achieved as a player it all means absolutely nothing when you become a manager.

"Most of my playing career was spent in the First Division, with Queen's Park Rangers, Crystal Palace and Coventry. I won 12 England caps and had the honour of captaining my country – which is the highest accolade that can be bestowed on any footballer. I had also been involved in coaching since I was 27 and had played under top managers like Alf Ramsey, Don Revie, Dave Sexton, Malcolm Allison and Terry Venables. So with a pedigree like that why did I have to worry about going into the Fourth Division?

Gerry Francis, manager of the month.

"I soon found out, getting the biggest culture shock of my life in what was a totally different world. I just could not believe what I had walked into. The players were on pathetic wages for a start, with £65 a week about the average. And it was the first time in my entire career I was working with people who could not pass a ball ten yards.

"The club needed a shake-up, with new players a matter of urgency, and when I took the job I was assured the money to buy them was there. But as it turned out there was no money. One of the things I have learned in my business career is to read a balance sheet and when I looked at Exeter's I soon realised the promises that had been made to me could never be kept.

"There was never a chance of it working out at St James Park for me and I was shown the door after nine months. But I learned some very harsh lessons and vowed never to make the same mistakes again.

"That's why when Bristol Rovers offered me the job three years ago I insisted on reading the balance sheet first. And having done it I did not think they would survive a year – that's how critical their financial situation was.

"But we are jumping ahead of the story. For at that time going back into management was the last thing on my mind. They say 'once bitten, twice shy' and I had certainly been bitten at Exeter.

"After leaving the Devon club I had brief spells as a player with Portsmouth, Cardiff and Swansea, before Bristol Rovers asked me to play for them. I was also doing some coaching at Wimbledon, where Dave Bassett was the manager at the time. And it was Dave who persuaded me to give management another go.

"Bassett approached me out of the blue to do some work with his players, after being impressed with what he had seen of me at Exeter. It's nice to know someone was! Exeter must have had the worst defence in the country at the time, and in one season gave away over 100 goals. I devised a system to tighten things up – and it worked. Wimbledon were in the Fourth Division at the time and when we played them Dave liked what he saw. He obviously remembered it, for a couple of years later he invited me to Plough Lane to work with his back four and midfield players.

"At that time I was coaching the Dons during the week and playing for Bristol Rovers on the Saturday – a situation not too many have found themselves in.

"When Bassett was offered the job at Watford – they wanted him to replace Graham Taylor who had moved to Aston Villa – he asked me to join him as full-time coach and initially I said 'yes' to the approach. Then Wimbledon went for Bobby Gould to take over from Bassett. That left a job vacant at Bristol Rovers and they asked me if I would take it on.

"At first I was not the slightest bit interested. For the painful memories of my experience at Exeter were still fresh in my mind. But I had a long chat with Dave Bassett, who persuaded me to give it another go. "I am delighted I listened to his advice, for the last three years have been an adventure I would not have missed for the world. It has been tremendous.

"When I took the job I did not imagine it would last this long. For, as I previously explained, the balance sheet provided such gloomy reading I could not see the club surviving a year. And the finances were not the only thing in a terrible state.

"People talk with pride about the marvellous spirit we have here now. They are right to do that, for what we have going is something very special. But it did not just happen – it had to be created, and it took time.

"When I first came morale was at rock bottom. Rovers were struggling in the Third Division and were the bookies' favourites to drop into the Fourth – a fate we managed to avoid.

"Spirit was non-existent. How can you expect anything else from a bunch of players who had become used to struggling season after season? Their record at Bath, the non-League ground where we have to play our home matches, was appalling. The lads seemed afraid of playing there and proved a push-over for most of the opposition. It's a different story now and anyone who takes anything away from Twerton Park has to work mighty hard for it.

"When I arrived here the players did not think they were capable of winning a match. That attitude has now changed considerably and if I left tomorrow the lads would still be convinced they could not lose one. So you can see the difference there is in the camp.

"The most important ingredient for success in football is consistency. And our form over the past two years proves we have achieved that. We lost only five of 46 League games last season – and that is an awesome record. And in the past two seasons we have never lost two games on the trot. That is something to be proud of – how many other clubs can say that?

"The top club in English football are Liverpool. They set the standards for everyone else to follow. They are the yardstick for everyone to measure themselves against. Consistency is the name of their game – and what we have achieved two grades lower in the League has reached their level.

"The financial situation here has meant I have not had money to throw around either for paying players, or buying them. My guys must have been among the lowest paid in the Third Division and 11 of the 13 were free transfers from other clubs.

"And even if I had *carte blanche* to go and sign players, can you imagine what a difficult job it would be to persuade them to sign for Bristol Rovers? Players, quite naturally, insist on looking over facilities before putting pen to paper. And I will be the first to hold my hands up and admit our facilities are hardly the best in the world.

"If a player wants to look round the ground that will be his new home I have to tell him, 'Sorry, son, we have not got one. We play on a ground borrowed from a non-League club.' If he wants to see the training ground I drive him over to Keynsham for a look around the pitches at the Cadbury's chocolate factory, who allow us the use of their facilities.

"Most clubs have a training ground that allows them to play reserve- or youth-team matches if necessary and provides indoor gym facilities. We are not in that privileged position. And if an intended signing asks to see the treatment room or kit room he will be told to take his pick from any of the Portakabins we have at Keynsham.

"That is what we are up against and that is what we have overcome to put this club back in the Second Division after an absence of nine years. For obvious reasons we have not got the best players in the world. But they have big hearts, honesty and are well organised.

"I have had to duck and dive and wheel and deal from the minute I walked in here to become the manager. And

I don't expect things to change now, even though we generated around £2 million last season from the sales of Nigel Martyn and Gary Penrice and the march to Wembley in the Leyland-Daf Cup final.

"I don't expect to be given any of that money for new players. I accept that it will be held back and put towards the money needed for the new ground, planned for the outskirts of the city. That is the big dream of everyone connected with the club. We have got to have our own stadium in order to get our identity back. But it is at least three years away yet – if it comes off at all. So it would be foolish for anyone to hold their breath.

"I have lost count of the number of players I have moved in and out since I came here. Martyn and Penrice – the big-money sales – are the ones most people are aware of because of the size of the fees and the impact they made with their new clubs, Crystal Palace and Watford respectively. But others like Tim Carter, Robin Turner, Paul Smith and Darren Carr went for fees that, although small, provided lifeblood for the club at the time.

"Penrice was the one attracting all the attention and the directors told me that if someone offered £5,000 for him I should bite their hand off. I resisted that because I wanted to switch him from a wide role to central striker and knew it would make him a much better player. In each of the two seasons after I did that Penrice got 24 goals to become one of the hottest properties in the game. And I was proved right, for when he did eventually move we got a hundred times more for him than the Board were prepared to accept in the first place.

"We had promised to let him go to a bigger club if he stayed and saw us through the previous season. So when Watford made their offer we kept our word.

"But it was a shock when Palace came for Martyn in the same week, and at first I did not want to let him go. He was playing non-League football for St Blazey in Cornwall and earning £100 a week outside the game. I offered him £105 for a full-time contract here . . . and a million-pound 'keeper was born!

"The £1 million Palace paid for the 'keeper who helped them to First Division respectability and the FA Cup final against Manchester United was a godsend and a club in Rovers' position could not turn it down. I was realistic enough to accept that. But it left me in a hole for the following Saturday's match, for I did not know where to turn to find a 'keeper to replace Martyn.

"In desperation I went to Pat Jennings, the former all-time great who played for Tottenham, Arsenal and Northern Ireland and set a world record of 119 international caps that was eclipsed by Peter Shilton during this summer's World Cup finals. I asked Pat, now 45, if he would consider coming out of retirement for a couple of weeks to help me out of a spot. But he had made his decision to quit at the top, would not be moved from it – and I respected him for that.

"Since then Brian Parkin has taken over in goal for us and done very well. He came from Palace as part of the Martyn deal – so we got a few bob and a capable replacement.

"Life at Rovers may have been tough, but it has most certainly never been boring. We have had our ups and downs but have all been big enough to forget about them and get on with the job of doing our best for the club we all care deeply about.

"I clashed with Geoff Twentyman and Paul Nixon in heavily publicised incidents. I could not ignore what they did, because both broke the rules and had to suffer the consequences. But it was all patched up and both played a significant part in our success last season.

"Of course you are going to have disagreements with the people you work with. Of course you are going to argue, explode and fall out from time to time. If that does not happen in a highly charged, emotional world like professional football something is drastically wrong. But you have got to take the action necessary at the time, then forget it. To carry grudges is to ask for trouble and it is important to treat players like men . . . not children. I learned that from Dave Sexton, manager of the England Under-21 team under Bobby Robson. Of all

Paul Nixon rises to power in a header.

the top managers I worked for, Dave influenced me the most of all. He treated me the way I wanted to be treated and I am the same with my players. I treat them the way I want to be treated. I don't believe in being called 'Boss' for a start. Gerry is my name and that will do nicely.

"I learned to be adaptable from Malcolm Allison. When he came to Crystal Palace for his second spell I had just completed the two most successful seasons of my career in midfield, playing well and scoring goals. Yet the first thing Malcolm said to me was 'I am going to play you as a sweeper'. I was horrified at the idea, thinking it was a waste of a midfield talent. But Mal was adamant – and it worked like a dream. He told me the top continental teams employed their best player as sweeper and I recall playing there and scoring in my first two games.

"During my playing career I was lucky enough to have operated in every position on the field – except goalkeeper. That gave me a good insight and working knowledge of everyone's role and I feel I can talk to any member of my team with some authority.

"I have been coaching since I was 27 and love that side of the game. I get a buzz from teaching people things that will help to make them better players. That is the most rewarding aspect of my job.

"I have always been a student of the game and paid very close attention to what is going on. I have never walked around with my eyes closed, unlike lots of players I have seen go through an entire career and never really learn anything. That is a tragic waste and to see as many players as I have passing up golden opportunities saddened me.

"When I was a player I loved to face the best, because it was a tremendous experience to test my skills against the finest in the world. My burning ambition was to reach the top of the tree – and with all due modesty I think I achieved that. After all I played for my country and had the honour of captaining my country. So you can't do much better than that.

"As a manager my ambitions are still the same. I would dearly love to pit my wits and footballing know-how against the greatest brains in the game. That would be a real thrill for me. And, who knows, now the ban on our clubs playing in Europe has, happily, lifted I may get the chance to do it.

"The ban from Europe for five bleak years was a real blow. It denied young players an important part of their soccer education and has been blamed when the England team have not done too well on the international stage.

"Our clubs had a tremendous record before the ban was imposed and I honestly believe they would have kept that impressive run going. I did some work for Sky TV during the summer, taking in the European club competitions and the World Cup. I watched the UEFA Cup final between Juventus and Fiorentina and you can't tell me that Liverpool would not have whipped the pair of them.

"I would have loved England to win the World Cup – and not for the obvious reason that I am a great patriot who wants us to be the best on this earth. An England victory –

More action from New Zealand's World Cup man Paul Nixon.

which at one time seemed a distinct possibility – would have left Margaret Thatcher's Tory Government red-faced with shame. And how I would have loved that after the shabby, disgraceful way they have treated the game I love.

"I honestly believe this Government would have no regrets at all if football went to the wall. I am convinced they would love to wipe our game off the face of the earth. That's why England would have really embarrassed them by winning the World Cup.

"There is no way they wanted us back in Europe – the stand they took for all those years proved that. But England's unexpected success in the World Cup forced their hand. They had to give in and recommend a return after the hysteria and acclaim that greeted England's march to the semi-final. That gave the whole country a lift and even this Government could not fly in the face of a public reaction like that.

"Despite their obvious loathing of football – or at least some of the people who follow it – the Government would have been quick to grab some of the glory and bask in it if England had gone on to win the trophy.

"They went on all the time about the hooligan problem in our game. Of course there is a problem. We all know that — and all hate what it has done to football in this country. But we are by no means the only ones with the problem. It also exists in Holland, West Germany and a growing number of other places. Yet these countries are allowed to continue playing in Europe and we don't hear calls from their own governments to sling them out.

"If there has been any incident involving our fans, our Government has been quick to seize on it and put us in a bad light. And I don't think a change of Sports Minister will change anything. In my opinion anyone will be an improvement on the disastrous Colin Moynihan. But whoever does the job is obviously only acting on orders from above."

Although Francis is bitter about the treatment football has had it has not diminished his love for the game that has been his life.

"Being a football manager is a young man's game. It is hazardous and stressful and the only certainty about it is that you will one day get the sack. If you don't take that fact on board the minute you become a manager, you will bring a lot of heartache to yourself."

Francis has already suffered that indignity at another club. With Rovers he is a god, and if he got the sack from there it would be one of the biggest shocks of all time.

Gerry has committed himself to the club for another season. It promises to be an eventful one for one of the brightest young talents in the business. And if it is to be his last one he intends to leave a lasting impression on the people of Bristol.

2

Denis Dunford

Chairman

B RISTOL ROVERS chairman Denis Dunford spent the summer fighting off another approach for outstanding young manager Gerry Francis – and counting the cash the club made from their march of triumph into the Second Division and the Leyland-Daf Cup final at Wembley.

There was nothing new in the fact that another club – in this case Aston Villa – wanted Francis. His exploits with Rovers have attracted national acclaim and several chairmen have been casting covetous eyes towards him. Villa wanted him to take over from Graham Taylor, who left to become the new manager of England. But when their chairman, Doug Ellis, asked for permission to speak to Gerry he was told in no uncertain terms to keep his hands off.

"At least Doug Ellis showed some ethics and made his approach in the proper way: through the front door. But the answer was still 'no'. We told him he could not speak to our manager," explained Dunford. "Gerry had signed a one-year contract with us only a week earlier and we were insisting that he honoured it. We know that other clubs had in the past gone round to the back door with unofficial approaches to him – and we have always fought all the way to keep him here. We have demonstrated to all and sundry how highly we value him. He has done a wonderful job for this club and it would have been silly to risk throwing all that away by giving Villa the go-ahead to talk to him.

Denis Dunford.

"When we told Gerry of our decision he accepted it well. We were well aware that he could have told us to stick our job and walked out of the door. After all, you can't force a man to do something he does not want to and contracts are only bits of paper. They do not have to be honoured.

"In situations like this it comes down in the end to whether a man has any integrity. And Gerry, happily, proved he has – although we knew that already. Being the sort of man he is, we would have been surprised – not to mention bitterly disappointed – if he had decided to tear up his 12-month agreement and take the Villa job."

Counting the cash Rovers raked in from a memorable season

was certainly a novel experience for Dunford, one that he enjoyed immensely. It was a refreshing change from lying awake at night wondering where the money was coming from to pay the players' wages. That was the grim position when Dunford became chairman of the club four years ago. Things were so bleak Rovers looked certain to fold up.

"The financial position was so grim few would have been the least bit surprised if the club had gone out of business. When I think back to those days I still don't know how we got through them," says Dunford. "When I took over as chairman we were £400,000 in debt and losing £5,000 a week. We had also just been forced to leave Eastville – so how on earth could we possibly clear debts like that with no assets? The club was insolvent – it was as simple as that. And directors trying to keep it afloat by pumping in their own money were warned they were putting other business interests at risk by knowingly trying to bale Rovers out.

"I discovered the full extent of the problem when I offered to do some book-keeping for the club before I joined the Board. I was horrified at what I found and told my son, Geoff, already a Rovers director, the club was in very serious financial trouble.

"Drastic action was needed and I took the harsh, but very necessary, steps when I took the chair at the ailing club. We needed £250,000 straightaway to avoid being taken to court for unpaid debts. The VAT man, the Inland Revenue, and the Stadium Company from whom we rented Eastville were all pressing for money owed to them.

"We had a training ground in a Green Belt area that was valued at £130,000 – just about half the money needed to get us out of immediate trouble. So obviously the sale of that would not have solved the problem. Then I hit on the idea of trying to find 20 people to each put in £12,500 and form a company to buy the training ground for £250,000, in the hope it would be worth more in around ten years' time so they could get their money back. In the event we managed to find 16 prepared to back the scheme and the directors made up the rest of the money. So we bought the ground and rented it to Rovers for £20,000 a year.

31

"Since then we have managed to get the excellent training facilities at Cadbury's in Keynsham for half that sum. So that was another big saving for us.

"When I became chairman I took on a completely new Board of directors and it was me who instigated the move to Bath City's Twerton Park ground, where we have played our home matches for the past four years. It was quite obvious we had to get out of Eastville, and Bath, 12 miles along the M4, has proved the ideal choice for us.

"Eastville, also a venue for greyhound racing, had been sold to the Stadium Company in 1947. Our lease expired in 1981 and they were prepared to renegotiate only for another five years, with compensation at the end of it. That was offered because they wanted us out in order to redevelop the site. Under the new agreement we were paying £60,000 rent, plus extras for floodlights, maintenance, duty electrician on match days and things like that.

"With our massive debts we were going nowhere fast. That situation could not be allowed to drift on and the rot had to be stopped. We would have had to get out of Eastville at the end of five years anyway – so I made the decision to go 12 months early.

"But where to? That was the big question. Sharing neighbours Bristol City's Ashton Gate ground was an early suggestion. But you did not need to be the brain of Britain to quickly realise that was a non-starter. As in most cities with two football clubs there is a great deal of rivalry and animosity between the fans. Our supporters would not have wanted to go there; City's would not have wanted us there.

"In fact, in the 1970s, when we had a fire at Eastville, we *did* play at Ashton Gate for three months. And our followers showed what they thought of it by boycotting the matches, simply refusing to watch us there.

"City were also aware of the problems. And although they agreed to let us share their ground they asked for an extortionate rent – a move made deliberately to price us out because they knew full well we would not be able to afford it.

"So Bath City it was and fortunately we have never looked

Skipper Vaughan Jones with the Third-Division Championship Trophy.

back since we moved in there. The beauty of going to Bath was that they are a non-League club and there would be no nastiness among the rival supporters.

"Savage economic measures were introduced as we began life in our new 'home'. It had to be done, for the very existence of the club was at stake. We were struggling in the Third Division at the time and I must be honest and admit I fully expected to see us drop into the Fourth. For everything – and everyone – expensive had to go as we cut to the bone and operated on a shoestring budget. All the top players went. No matter how vital to the club they were we could not afford them and they had to go.

"Attendances dropped – we expected that following the move from Eastville – but that was more than offset by the cut in running costs. We scraped by on part-time players, non-contract players – all sorts of odds and ends. I am full of admiration for the way people buckled down and got on with the job in very difficult circumstances. The hardship we were enduring forged a bond and brought an absolutely fantastic spirit. That has been one of the reasons behind the success we are enjoying now.

"Things took a turn for the better when Wimbledon came in for our manager, Bobby Gould. They wanted him to take over from Dave Bassett, who had replaced Graham Taylor at Watford. They gave us some compensation for taking a manager under contract to us, and Gould's first move was to buy defender John Scales off us for £80,000. That money was a godsend and things have steadily improved since we put it in the bank and brought in Gerry Francis as manager.

"What happened last season was a fairy tale as far as I am concerned. When I think of the trouble this club was in a few short years ago, when I think of how I used to lie awake at nights wondering where the money was coming from to pay the players' wages, I find it difficult to take in what is happening now. A return to the Second Division and an appearance in a glamour Wembley Cup final was the last thing on my mind as we struggled through the dark days looking for something, anything, to give us a bit of encouragement.

"We are making money now, instead of losing it. And that's the way it should be with any sensibly run business. Football is no different to any other commercial enterprise – it has got to be viable.

"Although the sun is shining on us now, I will never forget the days when the storm clouds were gathering overhead and I can promise they will never return. Too much hard work has gone into saving and reviving this club for it all to be thrown away. We have had enough of living on a knife-edge. From now on we live within our means.

"When you are on the floor, down and nearly out, it is amazing how people rally round you. There has been no shortage of volunteers to help out during our time of trouble, and it brought a wonderful spirit to the club. I just hope the fact we are now enjoying a little bit of prosperity does not spoil all that. Of course certain people are entitled to be rewarded now for sacrifices made in the past and we will do everything we can to make sure their contribution is recognised. All I hope is that some don't get greedy.

"At long last the future of this club is looking good. That is a wonderful feeling after spending a worrying time wondering whether we actually had a future. We have a superb manager in Gerry Francis, a fine set of players and go into the Second Division full of confidence and hope.

"Our average gate at Bath last season was 6,500. In our last season at Eastville it was just over 4,000. That is a big improvement and we hope to increase it even further next season.

"I am proud of all at Bristol Rovers for what they have achieved. It has been an incredible effort from everyone."

Denis Dunford runs a thriving dairy business in the West Country. He built it up with shrewd business acumen after buying one milk round when he left the RAF at the end of the war. He now has 40. He is determined to establish Rovers among the cream of football and the club owe a huge debt to the man who secured their future.

3

Vaughan Jones

Team Skipper

THE ROVERS' return to the Second Division is a dream come true for long-serving skipper Vaughan Jones. The 30-year-old Welsh boyo could not have asked for anything better if he himself had written the script for an exciting, memorable season. For Jones, a man of many parts and in his second spell at Bristol Rovers, is in his Testimonial season. And what a way to celebrate that – by roaring back to the Second Division after an absence of nine years!

Jones, a Welsh Youth and Under-21 International, thought his chance of a bit of glory had gone when Rovers were beaten in the Third Division play-offs 12 months earlier. But the tears of frustration he wept after Port Vale grabbed a late goal to beat Rovers 1-0 and clinch a place in the Second Division turned to tears of joy when Gerry Francis's team this time stormed home as champions.

"I suffered the best and worst moments of my footballing life in the space of a week at the end of last season," recalls Jones. "I was on a real high and everything looked smashing when we won at Fulham in our first play-off match. At that moment things could not have been better. Then we got beaten by an 86th-minute goal at Port Vale in the final – which meant they went into the Second Division and we were condemned to another season in the Third.

"I'm not ashamed to admit I cried like a baby after that disastrous result. I thought our promotion chance had gone forever and was devastated at the thought of spending the

Vaughan Jones.

rest of my career in the lower divisions. I was desperate to
taste a little bit of the sweet soccer-life before I quit and that
was the end of the world as far as I was concerned. I was
in such a sorry state that Des Bulpin, one of the coaches at
the club, rushed over to put his arms around me and try to
console me. That was a hopeless gesture at the time. I was
feeling so low, so sorry for myself, that no one could have
said or done a thing to ease the heartache I was suffering.
As Des did his best to help me I remember sobbing to him
'That's it. That's my big chance gone. That's the nearest I
will ever get to promotion and the opportunity will not come
again.'

"All those awful memories are still etched indelibly on
my mind. It seems like only yesterday they happened. So
winning promotion this time round as outright champions
is a sweet moment and more than makes up for the previous
year's disappointment. It is the first honour I have won after

13 years in the professional game and it just could not have come at a better time for me. To pull this off against the odds and get the whole area buzzing in my Testimonial season is an absolute dream.

"No one can say we did not deserve it. For to lose only five League games out of a tough programme of 46 is the stuff true champions are made of. Who can possibly deny that? All the lads were burning with the desire to make up for the previous year's sickening blow. They had just one target in mind – promotion – and went for it brilliantly. Obviously the mood was a little subdued when we reported back for pre-season training last July. The hurt and pain were still there from what had happened a few weeks earlier and the boys were still smarting from it. But once the season got under way we soon got that out of our systems and set about the job in hand – proving we were the best team in the Third Division and setting the standards for the rest to try and follow.

"The way we achieved that and the single-minded approach everyone showed is a credit to all connected with a club that has had more than its share of kicks in the teeth.

"The lads' attitude was brilliant all the way through. They could have sat back and got complacent after booking a Wembley appearance by reaching the final of the Leyland-Daf Cup – yet another milestone in a historic season for Bristol Rovers Football Club, but they did not. Promotion was the main aim, the top priority, and nothing was allowed to get in the way of that – not even a glamour game at one of the most famous places in world football. That took second place to the prized promotion place – clinched when we whipped local rivals Bristol City 3-0 at a packed, emotional Twerton Park on a crazy April evening.

"And to do that against the club who have always been considered the glamour outfit in the city of Bristol made it all the more sweet and satisfying. For obvious reasons they are the team we enjoy beating more than any other. The rivalry between our two clubs burns just as fiercely as it does on Merseyside, Manchester, Birmingham or North London with Tottenham and Arsenal. Our fans find it easier to go to work the day after we have put it across City. A result like that puts a bigger smile on their faces, an extra spring in their stride.

"But now the season is over and we have emerged as kings of the Division, everyone at Rovers is delighted City are coming into the Second Division with us. They earned that right by finishing runners-up to us to produce a great double for the city and the West Country and set up both sets of supporters for a happy summer break.

"That is a real shot in the arm for the folks down here. We look forward to going into battle against City in the Second Division this season and we know that some of football's so-called glamour teams won't look forward to taking us on. They have obviously been looking up road maps to find out where Bristol Rovers are. Once they do find us they will remember us . . . we can promise you that!

"Of course we are proud of what we have achieved. And we think we have every right to be, after overcoming massive problems to stay in business. I can think of a lot who would have been happy simply to tick over in our situation. We are made of sterner stuff than that and were determined to succeed to show what can be done if everyone is pulling in the same direction.

"I first joined Rovers in 1976, which makes me a member of that rare species . . . someone who actually played at Eastville! I left in 1982 to spend two years at Newport County. They had a great time while I was there, actually finishing just one point away from a place in the Second Division – heady success by their standards. Since then they have lost their place in the Football League and the club as everyone knew it folded and went out of business. What a tragedy that was for the game and the people of Wales!

"I then had six months at Cardiff, before returning to Rovers. So I have just completed my twelfth, and naturally most memorable season with them. In all those years I have, of course, seen many, many changes. But one thing has always stayed the same – the wages! The level of those has never changed!"

The wages factor nagged at Jones all through the summer of 1990 and led to big trouble for him when the players reported back for pre-season training in July. He went in and demanded a rise, was told he could not have what he was asking for . . . and was promptly slapped on the transfer list.

"It was a very sad way to get back to work and was the last thing I wanted to happen," claimed Jones. "I did not think I was asking for the earth – certainly for no more than players brought in to the club last season were getting. But we were nowhere near agreement on what the club insisted was their final offer to me.

"We all made sacrifices during the years when Rovers were in such deep financial trouble they were in grave danger of going out of business. Everyone accepted that and there were no complaints about the wages then. But it is all different now. Last season Rovers sold two players – Nigel Martyn and Gary Penrice – for £1.5 million. They won the Third Division championship and reached the Leyland-Daf Cup final at Wembley, pulling in a crowd of nearly 70,000. That all adds up to a lot of money and all I am asking for is a bigger slice of the cake. I don't think that is unreasonable and really hope we can work something out."

Rovers were rocked by the stance of a player they rate highly and do not want to lose. Club director Geoff Dunford explained: "We are not at all happy at the idea of letting him go. But he has turned down our final offer and there now seems no alternative for him. In our opinion he was asking for more than the earth. He wanted the solar system thrown in as well."

A parting of the ways would have been sad for Jones. Happily a solution was reached when Rovers came up with a last-ditch offer that Jones was satisfied with. It was still within their pay structure and Jones promptly made his peace and signed a new two-year contract. He was delighted that something was sorted out to break the deadlock.

"I love the club and everything it stands for. I have proved that by staying here for so long and it is marvellous to get some reward at last in the season that means the most to me – my Testimonial year.

"I have played in every position on the field – including

goalkeeper – in my time here. But in the last three seasons I have settled down at left-back. I have seen all sort of characters come and go. And I have seen better individual players than those here at the moment. But I have never, repeat *never*, seen a better team. The guys we have here now are a formidable unit because they play for each other and work for each other. We were a team in every sense of the word and that was the reason for our marvellous championship success.

"Even the loss of star players – Nigel Martyn to Crystal Palace and Gary Penrice to Watford – did not shake our confidence or composure. We simply brought in Brian Parkin and Carl Saunders to replace them and went about our business."

Vaughan is the proud owner of a Testimonial season T-shirt bearing the logo "Captain Gas". And he was certainly fired up as a thrilling season drew to a climax. With the title won and a Third Division championship medal proudly in his possession he then set his heart on the "double" – Leyland-Daf victory over Tranmere Rovers at Wembley. But his dream of leading his team up the steps to collect the trophy from soccer legend Sir Stanley Matthews turned into a nightmare as Tranmere won a hard fought match 2-1. Bristol Rovers turned angrily on referee Vic Callow, claiming he had denied them a legitimate penalty when Carl Saunders was pole-axed by Tranmere 'keeper Eric Nixon.

Shades of Port Vale 12 months earlier came flooding back as a bitterly disappointed Jones hurled his loser's medal away. It was picked up by Devon White and handed back to the Rovers skipper. The gesture may not have been appreciated at the time, but you can be sure that in years to come that medal will be one of Vaughan Jones's most prized possessions.

Pride of place, however, will go to the Third Division championship "gong" – one that Vaughan Jones worked so hard for . . . and waited so long for. After so many years at the "fag end" of the game it is great to see a true professional getting some reward . . . although not as much as he felt he was really worth – a burning issue that led him into conflict with Rovers.

4

Geoff Twentyman

Club Captain

G EOFF TWENTYMAN, the Rovers club captain, is bred from the very finest footballing stock. For his father, also Geoff, played for Liverpool – and you can't get a better pedigree than that.

Geoff junior followed in his father's footsteps by trying his luck at Anfield. But he never managed more than a few games in the reserves and was allowed to drift into non-League football with Chorley. More of that later. First comes the story of Geoff's exploits last season – the best one of his life.

It has to be called a tale of the unexpected, for Geoff did not expect to be involved with Bristol Rovers at all following a bust-up with manager Gerry Francis 12 months earlier. The flashpoint came when Rovers had qualified for the Third Division play-offs and Twentyman's brother decided to get married the day before the first of them, against Fulham.

"He wanted me to be his best man. And even though the manager said I could not have the time off so close to an important game there was no way in the world I was going to let my brother down. So I took off and went to his wedding," recalls Geoff. "It was not done as an act of defiance against the manager. I was in a difficult position and simply did what I felt was right at the time. My brother's wedding had to come first, because the family is the most important thing in life.

"I think Gerry understood my reasons for acting as I did.

Club captain, Geoff Twentyman.

But as the manager he could not simply let it go without taking action. And I accept he had to do that, for his concern was for Bristol Rovers. With him the club had to come first. He immediately suspended me and I was in dispute with the club for six weeks. I missed all four play-off games, an end-of-season trip to Spain, and thought my days at Rovers were over.

"I could not argue with what Gerry did. A manager has got to run the show and instil the discipline – I am the first to acknowledge that. And if I had been the manager and a player had done that to me I would have acted in exactly the same way to exercise my authority and show who was in charge.

"Despite that incident happening at what was a critical time for Bristol Rovers Football Club, Gerry and I never really fell out. There were no screaming or slanging matches, or any sulking afterwards. It was simply a clash of two very strong-willed people.

"However, after something like that happens – by no means an ordinary, everyday event in the lives of footballing folk – you begin to wonder if you have any future left with the club. Deep down I feared the worst and it would probably have been no great surprise to me if Gerry had told me I was no longer wanted and slapped me on the transfer list. But when I reported back for pre-season training – with more than a little trepidation – Gerry showed what a big man he was. He acted as though nothing had happened and the incident was completely forgotten. So I was able to get down to work and prepare for what turned out to be the most memorable season of my life.

"After going so close the previous year – remember we got beaten by Port Vale in the play-off final – we fancied our chances of doing well again. Our fans were convinced we could pull it off – and that put undue pressure on us. It does not automatically follow that if you have done well in one season you can keep the thing going. Football has a nasty habit of kicking you in the teeth and many's the time a team strongly fancied to win promotion finished up locked in a grim fight against relegation. So we were taking nothing for granted.

"We prepared as thoroughly as always and every man in the team gave 100 per cent every time he pulled on the blue-and-white-quartered jersey. We were all determined there would be no bitter taste of losing out in the play-offs this time. Our aim was to win promotion outright – and everyone connected with the club should be proud of the way it was achieved.

"To succeed in football it is vital to be consistent. You achieve nothing without that. And our level of consistency over the past two seasons has been tremendous. Don't forget we lost only five of 46 League matches last year. You can't get much more consistent than that and it is very satisfying as a professional footballer to look back on that impressive statistic.

"The season was, obviously, crammed with happy memories for me. But some things stand out more than others. Scoring a goal in our win at Preston was one. I enjoyed that, for I began my professional career at Deepdale. Beating Tranmere was another – for I was born and bred in Liverpool and it's nice to make your mark by toppling a team from your home-town area. Clinching promotion by beating neighbours Bristol City 3-0 at Twerton Park – and the scenes that followed – is something I will never forget. And winning at Blackpool to make sure of the Third Division title was an incredible experience. Over 5,000 of our fans made the journey to Bloomfield Road and they created a carnival atmosphere to roar us to the championship. The famous Blackpool lights looked dim compared to the blaze of colour our fans created on the Bloomfield Road terraces that day. At that moment every one of us was delighted. We had done exactly what we set out to do nine months earlier, so we would not have wanted to swop places with anyone. Even the disappointment of losing to Tranmere in the final of the Leyland-Daf Cup at Wembley could not take the shine off a memorable season. Promotion, after all, had been the top priority.

"I must admit to feeling very low after the Wembley defeat. Two dozen of my family and friends had travelled down from Merseyside for the big day and as an exiled Scouser it hurt to lose to the boys from across the river in Birkenhead. But I soon got that out of my system and now look forward to sampling life in the Second Division. That's a great prospect for a 31-year-old, who thought the good things in football life were passing him by. It certainly justifies my decision to throw up a secure job in banking to go full-time at the age of 24. A lot of people thought I was taking a risk at that time of life – but I have never regretted it for a second. My philosophy is that you only live once and if the chance you have dreamed of comes along you have got to go for it. I did and it has worked out brilliantly for me.

"With my dad being a Liverpool player I grew up with the very best and, naturally enough, my only ambition was to follow him into professional football. I never made the grade at Anfield, so drifted into non-League football with Chorley and a job in banking after getting two A levels. But I still had a strong yearning to play full-time football, although people whose opinions I respected warned me I would be mad to give up long-term security to go into something as notoriously hazardous as professional soccer. I knew there was a lot of sense in what they said, for the casualty rate in football is very high. But when the big moment came and I was offered the chance to sign for Preston it was, as they say, 'no contest'.

"If I did give up a secure, well-paid job to try my luck in football I knew I *might* live to regret it. But if I turned down the opportunity I had waited all my life for I *knew* I would. After all, this was something I had always wanted. I was no longer a starry-eyed kid – I was 24, an age when very few people get an offer to turn professional. It was a dream come true. So I took the plunge and can honestly say I have never regretted it for one minute. I had three happy years at Deepdale before Bristol Rovers signed me and I am now in my fourth season with them.

"When my playing days are over – and at 31 there is a lot of life in the old warhorse yet – I want to move into the coaching and management side of the game. And that is where working under Gerry Francis will come in very handy and help me realise yet another ambition. Gerry is an absolutely outstanding coach and I have never met anyone who is as knowledgeable on the game. His is an all-round knowledge. Whether he is talking about goalkeepers, midfield players or front men he is an expert on the subject and his advice is always first-class. He deserves a bigger stage on which to demonstrate his abilities, for he is one of the most brilliant brains in the business. We are all delighted he has decided to stay with Rovers. It was a big boost to us all when Aston Villa were refused permission to talk to him. We all think the world of him and it would have been a crushing blow to lose the man who has done so much for us.

"Despite the wonderful success we enjoyed last season, despite the fact we pushed our more affluent neighbours Bristol City into second place in the table, we know we are still the city's poor relations.

"How can it be any other way when we have no ground and no training ground? Until that is put right the position will never change.

"Plans are being discussed at the moment for a new ground in the Mangotsfield area of the city. It could take years to become reality – but the day can't come soon enough for everyone with the interest of Bristol Rovers at heart. And that includes anyone with even the slightest acquaintance with the club. Rovers are an outfit who get to you; it does not take long to form an attachment to them and I know that whatever I do for the rest of my life, wherever I go, they will always be a part of me.

"The club has finally emerged from a long, dark tunnel and there is hope for the future at long last. There is so much to look forward to now and you can take it from me we will all be going for it in a big way."

One event Geoff was happy enough to miss was his brother's first wedding anniversary. That fell on the day Rovers played Tranmere in the Leyland-Daf Cup final at Wembley . . . so there was not the slightest danger of him going missing this time!

5

Ian Alexander

IAN ALEXANDER considered himself lucky to be alive to play a part in Rovers' promotion push after being involved in a horrific incident three years ago. The 27-year-old full-back almost died when he swallowed his tongue in a Sunday afternoon FA Cup-tie against non-League Fisher Athletic. Only quick-thinking by club physio Roy Dolling saved his life.

Dolling, who has now done this three times, was on the scene quickly to whip out Alexander's false teeth and move his tongue to free the air-passage and get him breathing again. At the time no one in the crowd realised just how serious the situation was. But Alexander knows he probably owes his life to Dolling.

"I don't remember a thing about the incident. All I can recall is getting a bang on the head and waking up in hospital. But I was told later what Roy had done and will, of course, always be grateful to him. It taught me a sharp lesson about playing football with my false teeth in. Since that day they have been left in the dressing-room before every match."

Alexander has found his feet and his best form at Rovers after switching from winger to full-back. In his previous position he enjoyed no more than a moderate career with Rotherham, Morton and Motherwell. And he spent a year in Cyprus before signing for Rovers four years ago.

All that the father of two sons, Ricky and Andrew, knew about full-backs before joining Rovers was that they were the people who kicked wingers like him.

Ian Alexander.

"My initial reaction when I was asked to play there was that it would be nice to get a little bit of my own back for the treatment they had dished out to me over the years," he says.

"Someone, namely manager Gerry Francis, could obviously see something in me I could not see in myself. But I was prepared to give it a go, for I had absolutely nothing to lose. And I'm very glad I did now. For although it felt strange making the switch at first, I am happy at full-back now and much prefer playing there. It has worked out well for me and the team, who have done wonders in view of all the problems we have faced in recent years. Beating neighbours Bristol City and winning promotion on the same night was without doubt the sweetest moment of my life. It was a tremendous occasion – one I will never forget.

"I must admit that promotion seemed no more than a fanciful hope as the problems piled up for us. Money was scarce here and we knew the club had to sell to survive, but I still felt really low when Gary Penrice and Nigel Martyn went in quick succession. Crystal Palace paid £1 million for Martyn – at that time a British record for a goalkeeper, and he repaid them by getting them to the FA Cup final against Manchester United. Watford gave £500,000 for Penrice, who wasted no time in scoring goals for them. And although it brought badly-needed money into this club I think we all felt a bit flat that two key players had been allowed to leave. But we reacted to it in just the right way – by pulling together and working that bit harder to make sure their departure did not wreck our promotion chances.

"The fact we are football's poor relations – with no ground and a borrowed training ground – has forged stronger links within the squad and made us more determined to defy the odds. I think we all have every right to be proud of the way we have overcome every obstacle put in our way.

"We are not kidding ourselves that life will get any easier because of what we achieved last season. For the bottom line is we still have no ground and no training ground. We will still be playing our home games at Twerton Park, which effectively means every match is an away fixture for us. And things will be even tougher, for we are now coming up against opposition from the Second Division, and with teams like Newcastle, Sheffield Wednesday and West Ham we know what we are up against. But teams like that are certain to pack them in when they come down here to play us and we are all looking forward to the challenge.

"The best news of all during the summer was the fact that Gerry Francis was staying with us. In view of the marvellous job he has done here it was obvious bigger clubs wanted him and it was no surprise to anyone when Aston Villa made a move to get him as replacement for new England boss Graham Taylor. The Bristol Rovers Board did everyone a favour when they refused Villa chairman Doug Ellis permission to speak to him and it is great to know Gerry is with us for at least another season. He has organised us well, got us playing to our strengths and made us feel that anything is possible. So we are not afraid of taking the step into the Second Division.

"What happened last season was sheer magic, a marvellous experience for everyone connected with Bristol Rovers. But that's history now. All that matters is the new season . . . and it is one we are all looking forward to immensely."

6

Brian Parkin

Goalkeeper

TAKING OVER from a million-pound goalkeeper, one of the biggest crowd favourites at the club, was no laughing matter. But even Brian Parkin will now admit he took things a bit too far when he joined Bristol Rovers to replace Nigel Martyn.

Martyn started a rapidly accelerating trend last November. He became Britain's first million-pound 'keeper when he moved from Bristol Rovers to Crystal Palace. That was a forbidding figure all other managers had refused to pay for a man to be their last line of defence. Even the great Peter Shilton, holder of a world record of 125 caps, never cost money like that.

Since Martyn became the trailblazer and founder-member of that exclusive million-pound club others have quickly followed suit. Arsenal boss George Graham broke through the barrier to sign David Seaman from Queen's Park Rangers; Graham got his money back when he moved John Lukic on to Leeds United; then big-spending Manchester City manager Howard Kendall paid £1 million for Tony Coton from Watford.

But Martyn was the first into that unknown territory. And that made the job of replacing him all the more difficult for Parkin – a 25-year-old Scouser, who came from Palace as part of the deal.

"I did not enjoy it at all at first. I was very nervous at the idea of taking over from Nigel, a great favourite with the fans down here and a player they did not want to see leave the club. I put pressure on myself by thinking it would be very difficult to step into the boots of a popular player like that. But the rest of the lads here were brilliant in helping me to

52

An acrobatic save from Brian Parkin.

settle down. They told me to relax and just be myself. They emphasised that, fine 'keeper though Nigel was, he was by no means irreplaceable and assured me they had the utmost faith in me to carry on the good work. That sort of thing has obviously been the secret of Rovers' great success. The lads are all in it together and all pull in the same direction. Their help was invaluable to me."

The Rovers players may have been quick to give Parkin all the help they could to make sure he settled quickly into his new surroundings. They were also very quick to give him unmerciful stick for his attitude and approach when he first arrived.

"I suppose I was a little bit serious and withdrawn. And that stood out in a dressing-room used to happy smiling faces," recalls Parkin. "It must have been hard for the lads to take and they wasted no time in giving me some nicknames. 'Mr Glum' and 'Gloomy' were among the more polite ones and I must admit I can now see their point. I did have a few moans when I first came here and that was something the rest of the dressing-room were not used to."

Parkin astonished his team-mates when Rovers played Walsall in the area semi-final of the Leyland-Daf Cup. He saved three spot kicks in the penalty shoot-out . . . and was actually seen to smile.

"At least, we think that's what he was doing. But it was such an unusual occurrence the rest of the lads were looking for a camera to capture the moment on film. It was that rare," jokes club skipper Geoff Twentyman. "Brian got some stick about that incident, which provided great wind-up material for the rest of us. But he took it well and we are all grateful for the way he settled down and played a vital role in our success story.

"Of course he was worried about taking over from Nigel Martyn. That was understandable, for Nigel was big news when he became Britain's million-pound 'keeper and Brian knew how popular he was in these parts. But we did all we could to put him at ease and he soon got over his fears to become an important – and happy – member of the squad."

If Parkin had worries about the move in the first place, he certainly has none now. He is happily settled in a flat in Bath and regards the move to Rovers as the best thing that ever happened to him. He was stuck in a rut at Palace, going nowhere fast. And his desire to get away was increased following a bust-up with manager Steve Coppell, on one of the blackest nights in the history of Crystal Palace.

"I was back on my native Merseyside last September, when Palace played Liverpool at Anfield. And they won't thank me for reminding them that was the night Palace suffered a humiliating 9-0 defeat," he says. That was the game that was to have profound repercussions for me – although I did not know it at the time. It was the game that convinced Coppell he needed a new goalkeeper. And when he decided Nigel Martyn was the man he wanted that gave me the green light to come to Rovers. So I have cause to thank him now – although I did not have at the time.

"I had gone to Liverpool to see the game and my folks, who live across the river in Birkenhead. But Coppell told me I should have been back in London preparing for a reserve game and hit me with a fine. Of course I was not very happy about that and knew I just had to get away from Selhurst Park. Although I had played in 24 matches in the season that brought Palace promotion from the Second Division – sharing the goalkeeping duties with Perry Suckling – I was completely frozen out when they reached the First Division. I made only one appearance – against Luton – after the deal for Martyn had been agreed.

"Coming here was a brilliant move for me and I could never have dreamed the season would end on such a high for me, with a Third Division championship medal and a Wembley appearance.

"Even the fact that we got beaten 2-1 by Tranmere – and can you imagine the stick my Scouser family gave me over that! – did not spoil things too much. We played well, were unlucky to lose and I had appeared at Wembley. And lots of far better players than me go through their entire career and never do that.

"I was a bit upset during the summer when Graham Taylor left Aston Villa to become the new manager of England. For it was obvious to anyone that our boss, Gerry Francis, would be high on Villa's wanted list. So it turned out and I breathed a huge sigh of relief when the Rovers Board refused Villa permission to speak to him and insisted he honoured the one-year contract he had signed a month earlier. Gerry, being the kind of man he is, was happy to do that and I am delighted he will be leading us in the Second Division this season. He is the best manager I have ever worked for, and for a man who never played in goal he knows an incredible amount about the position.

"He is also a decent human being, a man you can go to if you have any personal problems. I know from personal experience he will do all he can to help you out. Rovers did well to get him in the first place and have done even better to keep him. We all intend to repay him in the best possible way . . . with success on the field."

7

Nigel Martyn

Former Goalkeeper

N O ONE got more pleasure from Rovers' triumphant march to the Third Division title and the Leyland-Daf Cup than former 'keeper Nigel Martyn. He became Britain's first million-pound goalkeeper when he was sold to Crystal Palace last November. And the doubting Thomases reckoned that when Nigel and Gary Penrice – sold within a week of each other – went, so did Rovers' hopes of glory. Those that stayed behind proved the doubters wrong. And Martyn – who chalked up an FA Cup final appearance for Palace against Manchester United – was delighted.

"After leaving I followed Rovers' fortunes very closely. Theirs was the first result I looked for when I got back to the dressing-room following our own game every Saturday and I keep in touch with the players," revealed Martyn.

"Obviously I did not get much chance to watch them play, because I was invariably in action for Palace myself at the same time. But there was no way I was going to miss their Wembley appearance against Tranmere Rovers. I would have bought a ticket and joined the Rovers fans in the crowd if necessary. But Radio Bristol asked me to do the summaries for them during the match, so I watched it from the commentary box.

"I was so pleased for the lads, who had achieved so much against all the odds. When most people reckoned they would go out of business they responded by going instead into the

Nigel Martyn.

Second Division and to a Wembley Cup final.

"Gary and I had to be sold to keep the club solvent, to ease a crippling financial situation. Everyone accepted that – but we did not share the gloom that surrounded our departure. There was a feeling among the fans that Rovers had sold their hopes of winning anything when they sold us. But we did not go along with that and are both very happy to be proved right.

"I knew the lads had enough ability to go on and win promotion from the Third Division. I also knew the loss of two players would spur the rest to dig in and fight even harder – and that is exactly what happened.

"The spirit at Rovers is superb. If any club in the country has a better one they are very lucky, and for the boys to achieve this after all they have been through is amazing. I can't speak too highly of them.

"The hardship they endured for several years has forged a great bond in the dressing-room. The wages there are not the best in the world – but they are all the club can afford and everyone gets the same. There were no stars, all got treated the same and that made sure there was no resentment. When you are all in a situation together and pulling hard for the club the worst thing you can discover is that someone is getting special treatment. That did not happen at Rovers. And that is why everyone gave 100 per cent every week to do their bit for the club. It really was like one big, happy family.

"I was not aware of Rovers' financial problems when I signed for them from Cornish club St Blazey in July 1987. And even if I had been it would have made not the slightest difference, for I was not going very far playing in the South-Western League and the chance to join a Football League club was just too good to turn down. I could not have made a better choice. Not only are Rovers a smashing little club, they have one of the most outstanding managers in the country in Gerry Francis. He has done a superb job for the club and his knowledge astounded me. He can talk to every player about his job and suggest ways of improving his game – even goalkeepers! That is unusual for an outfield player, but he certainly helped me develop into a 'keeper good enough to move into the big time for a very big fee.

"I was sad to leave Rovers. For, despite the hardship there, it was a very happy little club. But they needed the money and, like any footballer, I was ambitious to play in the First Division.

"It worked out well for me – with Palace consolidating in the First Division and reaching the FA Cup final. It also worked out well for Bristol Rovers – which makes me one very happy man. I wish them well for the future and will always follow their fortunes with close interest and feel part of a club it was a pleasure to play for."

8

Gordon Bennett

Former Chief Executive

IGHTING THE cause for Bristol Rovers as part-time scout, Youth
Development Officer and Chief Executive over a period of 17
years left Gordon Bennett physically and mentally drained. He
had given everything he had in a bid to keep the financially stricken
club alive. So when new chairman Denis Dunford and his Board took
over Bennett called it a day in May 1986.

"I was whacked, totally drained by all the years of scrimping
and scraping and worrying whether the club would survive.
To say all my years with Rovers were eventful would be
putting it mildly," says Bennett – now Youth Development
Officer at Norwich City, where he has linked up again with
former Rovers player-manager David Williams.

"I was still Chief Executive at Rovers when the new Board
took over and the move to Bath City took place. But once the
dust had settled and economic measures had been imposed
to safeguard the future of the club I knew it was time for me
to go.

"All the efforts of the previous years had taken a heavy
toll. It took a lot out of me and I knew I could not continue
making the contribution I had been doing to the Rovers
cause. So, convinced that Rovers had now taken steps to
keep the Receiver out once and for all, I decided it was
time to recharge my batteries with a long rest then look
for a fresh challenge. I found that with a job as secretary at

Gordon Bennett.

West Bromwich Albion. I held that post for three years and came to Norwich 12 months ago. But Rovers will always be part of me. How could it ever be any other way after working for them for so many years? I am a West Country lad anyway and loved that club so much I started working for them on a part-time basis.

"The club is in very good hands now. Chairman Denis Dunford and his fellow directors are a prudent bunch who will make sure Rovers live within their means in future. They will not allow the overspending that has been sanctioned here in the past and was the root cause of all Rovers' financial traumas. They care deeply about the club and all pumped in their own money in a bid to save it. Without their actions Bristol Rovers would now be no more than a memory.

"When Mr Dunford took over he imposed the most savage cuts you could imagine. It was brutal but it had to be done to keep the club alive. Everything unnecessary went, everything too expensive went and Bobby Gould, the manager at the time, was given a budget of just £125,000 for wages for his entire squad. If any manager in the Football League was working on a lower figure than that I would not have liked to be in his shoes. It was harsh, it was unpleasant. But everyone accepted it had to be done to prevent the club from folding, so all buckled down and got on with the job.

"The first miracle happened when Gould kept the club in the Third Division in season 1986/7 – the first year of the move to Bath. We were most people's favourites to go down and it would have been no great surprise to anyone if we had dropped into the Fourth. But Bobby and the boys battled for their lives out on the pitch every week and managed to preserve our Third Division status. That was a tremendous boost for everyone and provided a platform to work from. Relegation to the Fourth Division after everything else that had happened would have been a really bitter blow and the survival act proved to everyone it was not all gloom and doom.

"Since then, of course, Gerry Francis has moved in and performed a miracle almost every day. The job that man has done for Rovers is absolutely incredible and no praise can be too high for him. It shows how much he cares for the club that he has resisted the chance to move to bigger things by signing a new one-year contract. Rovers know they are lucky to keep him, for he is certainly one of the most highly rated managers in the game.

"The money worries came to a head in the mid-1980s, when Rovers had to leave Eastville and sell their training ground just to make sure they did not go to the wall. But the problems go back a lot further than that. In fact, the club have been in 'intensive care' for as long as I can remember. And the policy of successive Boards in sanctioning overspending did not help the cause one little bit.

"I can recall that soon after I became Chief Executive in 1980, I went to a Board meeting and was told we needed £100,000 in a month to keep the club alive. For a club like Bristol Rovers to find that sort of money – quite a lot ten years ago – was not an easy task. But we managed it and one more crisis had passed. There were to be plenty more in the intervening years and how we kept the wolf from the door and avoided having the Official Receiver called in I will never know.

"All the troubles stem from the fact that Rovers did not own the Eastville ground that was their home. They leased it from the greyhound company, who thereby called the tune. They were not in business to be benevolent to their tenants – a Football League club which brought prestige to the city of Bristol. And once the M32 was laid – a motorway that was virtually right above the ground – the writing was on the wall.

"That suddenly made Eastville a prime site for development and the pressure went on to get us out so it could be developed. We bowed to the inevitable and went a year before we needed to – knowing we would have to get out anyway – and the site is now a trading estate. The greyhound track is still in place, to provide memories of all the years Rovers spent at Eastville for any fan who drives past.

"The move to Bath was the lifesaver for the club. Going to Bristol City's Ashton Gate and sharing with our bitter rivals was out of the question. Everyone knew that. The fans of both clubs would never have stood for it for a start. We explored the possibility, but realised very quickly to have tried that would have been asking for trouble.

"There was nowhere else in the city to play, so we simply had to move out. Fortunately we managed to convince our fans the very existence of the club depended on the switch to Bath and they accepted it. We managed to hold on to the bulk of our support. We did not lose a huge chunk of our following like Charlton did when they quit the Valley to go and share with Crystal Palace at Selhurst Park. That move caused a rebellion. Ours was accepted. Our supporters were aware of the huge problems we faced and played their part in driving a dozen or so miles along the M4 to continue to support us.

"What happened at Rovers was certainly an adventure. But it is not one I would care to experience again. It definitely left a mark on me — one I will never forget. But I am delighted they are back on an even keel at last and making money, instead of losing it year after year. I am delighted for a lovely little club that they are back in the Second Division and enjoyed a glamour day out at Wembley last May. The people running the club now will look after it and they have one of the brightest young managers in the League. What more could anyone want? I enjoyed my time there immensely and wish them well for the future."

9

Roy Dolling

Physiotherapist

ROY DOLLING is walking around Bristol these days with a smile on his face, a spring back in his step and his head held high. Bristol Rovers' physiotherapist and Youth Development Officer is proud to face the public again. And that makes a nice change from being fearful of how they might react to someone belonging to the city's "bits and pieces" football club.

Rovers have always been the poor relations in the sport-mad West Country city. They are the ones with no home to call their own, while neighbours City have facilities which would – indeed have – graced the First Division.

Rovers have been regarded with sympathy and pity because of their financial plight and long-serving, loyal club people like Dolling have been upset at not being taken seriously. But all that changed dramatically last May, when Bristol Rovers produced an emphatic reply by winning the Third Division championship and reaching the final of the Leyland-Daf Cup, losing 2-1 to Tranmere Rovers in controversial circumstances. Those exploits gave Dolling the sweetest moments in his 16 years with Rovers and he expects them to now get the respect they deserve.

"After this perhaps people will start to take us seriously instead of laughing at us – which has been the case all too often in the past here. This club has worked a miracle in achieving success against enormous odds and it will be a tragedy if we don't get the credit we deserve.

"In view of all that has happened here – being forced to

Roy Dolling.

leave the Eastville Stadium, and having to sell the training ground and our best players to survive – I did not think it was possible. I don't think too many others did either and it seems fantastic that a club threatened with going out of business is instead going into the Second Division. That gives me a marvellous feeling. Obviously it is the most enjoyable time in all my years with the club. For the first time in my experience we have cause for optimism. We seem to have a future at last. We are in the black at the bank and it's great to be making money instead of losing it week after week and worrying just how long the club can keep going.

"Gerry Francis has done a wonderful job since taking over as manager three years ago and this club owes him a huge debt. As a coach he is brilliant – second to none – and his man-management is very good. He is one of that rare breed of managers who appoint people to do other jobs and let them get on with it. There is no interference from him. Of course he wants to know what's going on and asks questions, but when it comes to players' fitness the final decision is mine. A lot of managers are under pressure to get players on the pitch, regardless of whether they are 100 per cent fit or not and it is common in football for someone to be forced into action when he should be on the treatment table. That does not happen with Gerry. We talk about it . . . then he is happy to leave the final decision to me. And that is good from my point of view – for it shows the manager has complete faith in the staff working for him."

Dolling has become one of the most respected physios in the game after *three times* rescuing players in danger of choking after swallowing their tongues. Defender Aiden McCaffrey did it after a collision with 'keeper Phil Kite in a game against Southend. Ian Alexander was the victim when Rovers played non-League Fisher Athletic in a Sunday afternoon FA Cup-tie at Twerton Park. And the most recent one was Bristol City full-back John Bailey. Prompt action by the vigilant Dolling got him quickly to all three to prevent what could have been tragedies. Now he gives lectures on the vital importance of having expert medical attention at sporting events.

"A survey down here showed that more people take part in active sport in the Bristol area than any other part of the country. And what I see on my local travels saddens and frightens me," Dolling claims.

"A kid playing football on a parks pitch will go down injured and someone will run on to him with a bucket and sponge – and not the slightest idea what he is doing. These people are well meaning, there is no doubt about that. But their first-aid knowledge is probably zero and they could end up doing more harm than good.

"The way football is being played now increases the risk to people, in my view. The ball is in the box more, in the air more – so that inevitably increases the risk of head injuries. This trend worries me a great deal and I am trying to do my bit to make sure responsible, qualified treatment is at hand to look after players in trouble."

Dolling joined Rovers as the reserve-team physio on a part-time basis in 1974, after serving 32 years in the printing industry. He eventually joined the staff full-time, worked with Parkway Juniors, the club's nursery team, and had the satisfaction of helping to develop nuggets like Gary Mabbutt and Gary Penrice.

When the financial problems really came to a head Dolling had to go – sacrificed on the altar of economic necessity. That was in the mid-1980s and when a devastated Dolling walked out of the door at Eastville – still the Rovers home at that time – he vowed he would never return.

"Bobby Gould took me on full-time. David Williams replaced him as manager and let me go. I left the club just before David himself went, and was told there was not enough money and that the club could not afford me. That was a shattering blow, because by this time I had become the Rovers Youth Development Officer. I took over that job from Gordon Bennett, who had become Chief Executive. When I was told I had to go I was so upset I vowed I would never go back into full-time professional football. I would never go back to the game, for after what happened I saw no point in carrying on. In my opinion the development of youth talent is the most important job at a club – certainly a club in the lower divisions of the Football League. Everyone is feeling the squeeze now. The financial pressure is increasing and only the élite few can afford big transfer fees. So it is becoming vitally important to get out and find your own young talent. I had worked very hard for Rovers. I had put a lot into the club, developing stars of the future like Mabbutt and Penrice, and to be told I was no longer wanted because they could not afford me, hurt. I thought to myself, 'Right, that's it. If this is what professional football is all about I don't want to know. They can leave me out of it.'

"Then David Williams left to resume his playing career with Norwich City. Bobby Gould came back for his second spell as manager and wanted me to return to the club. My response to that was an abrupt 'No chance' for I was still angry at my earlier treatment. But he would not take no for an answer and I went back part-time. When Bob left for Wimbledon in 1987 Gerry Francis became manager and demanded that I return full-time.

"He went as far as sending chairman Denis Dunford and his director son Geoff round to my house to ask what I would want to go back to Rovers. I told them a five-year contract . . . and a salary I never dreamed they would agree to. To my astonishment they did – so here I am working for Bristol Rovers again and loving every minute of it. The move to Bath four years ago and the success we enjoyed last season has transformed the club and the future is looking good.

"The top priority for everyone is a new ground. We hope to have an all-seater stadium in the Mangotsfield area of the city – and I just hope and pray it comes off, for it will make my job a lot easier if we have some proper, decent facilities again.

"Can you imagine the job I have now persuading promising youngsters to join a club with no ground and no training ground? There is not much at the moment to impress the boys, or their parents. Imagine a kid looking round the facilities at, say, Manchester United, Liverpool, Arsenal or Tottenham then coming here. After all those glamour clubs have to offer I can show him three Portakabins at the bottom of a field and three lights on a pole to train them under in the evenings. Big deal! That does not make life any easier and I cannot wait for the day we get our own ground again. It will certainly improve our chances of persuading youngsters to come here.

"Another dream I have is to get the best young talent in the area to sign for Rovers – and to keep them here. In the past this club have been forced to sell their best players to keep going. Wouldn't it be great to go into the First Division for the first time ever with a team of Bristol boys? An impossible dream? Who knows? After what has been achieved here recently against all the odds who can say anything is impossible?"

10

Ray Kendall

Kit Man

RAY KENDALL has been around the Bristol Rovers scene much longer than anyone else . . . 40 years, to be precise. And Ray of the Rovers has seen it all and done it all in a variety of jobs since first linking up with the club in July 1950. There was nothing more they could do to either surprise or impress him. Or so the loyal 60-year-old thought. The stirring events of the last unforgettable season changed all that and brought a tear to the eye of the man who has given most of his life to the cause of Bristol Rovers.

"Winning the Third Division championship in such fine style and going on to the Leyland-Daf Cup final at Wembley was an incredible achievement in view of all the problems we have faced," says Kendall. "I would not have thought that was possible – especially after selling our best two players, Nigel Martyn and Gary Penrice, with less than half the season gone. What we went on to achieve was beyond anyone's wildest dreams. To lose only five matches in a tough, demanding League-programme of 46 games was a fantastic performance.

"I can't speak too highly of the players. They are a superb bunch with probably the best team-spirit I have known in all my years here. We have had better players here, there is little doubt about that. The team in the 1950s – the last one to win the Third Division championship – for instance. They had performers like

Ray Kendall.

Harry Bamford, Geoff Fox and Geoff Bradford, among the finest this club have ever had. But even they could not have pulled off what the lads of 1989/90 did.

"Back in the 1950s we had a settled background, a home ground at Eastville to play on, a training ground and no money worries. In short, all the things you would expect a properly run Football League club to have. The boys who battled so brilliantly last season had nothing. They faced a journey to Bath to play their home games and had to train on a sports ground borrowed from a local chocolate factory. I wonder how many other teams could have conquered all that and still come up trumps? Not many, I am willing to bet.

"At the top of the League ladder in this country we hear a lot about pampered, overpaid stars having everything done for them and living the life of luxury. A few of

70

them should come down here and see what our lads have to put up with. They have knuckled down and got on with their job in magnificent style and I am full of admiration for them. They certainly made me a proud and happy man.

"I have seen all sorts of characters come and go since I first joined this club as a part-time match-day steward all those years ago. I have laughed with them, cried with them and have a fund of wonderful memories. But the best one of the lot is the day out at Wembley the boys gave me for that Leyland-Daf Cup final against Tranmere Rovers last May. What a marvellous experience that was, one that will last me for the rest of my days. After 40 years of working in Second and Third Division dressing-rooms, to actually be involved at Wembley is a dream come true. Just as it is every footballer's dream to play at the famous old stadium, so it is every kit manager's dream to lay out the gear in a dressing-room there. I fulfilled a lifetime's ambition when I did that.

"The drive from our overnight hotel to the stadium was just as I imagined it to be – just as I had watched other teams making the journey when I took in FA Cup finals on TV, year after year. And walking up the tunnel before the game to see over 30,000 of our fans having the time of their lives brought a lump to my throat. That was an amazing sight.

"I also had the great thrill of meeting a lot of celebrities before the match in what proved to be an emotional experience for me. The only unhappy note was struck when the lads failed to win the match. But they gave it all they had in a very close encounter and with any luck could have become the first team ever to win the lower Leagues double – Third Division title and Leyland-Daf Trophy."

That glamour day at the most illustrious stadium in English football was a million miles away from the normal working environment of Kendall, the Rovers kit man who describes himself as the club's 'gofer'. He was taken on the full-time staff 12 years ago after being made redundant from local cigarette manufacturer W. D. & H. Wills.

And Rovers will never get a more willing or loyal servant. He does anything for them.

"Kit man is my official title. But my duties extend a lot further than that. I am, in effect, the 'gofer' – if anyone wants anything I go for it," Kendall says. "If the manager wants petrol, a service on his car or anything else, I take care of it. If physio Roy Dolling wants any medical supplies I get them.

"In fact I start my day with a visit to the Crest Hotel at Hambrook. I am there at eight o'clock every morning to pick up a box of ice for Roy. He needs it for the treatment of injured players and it has to be collected like that because we have no water supply at the training ground.

"Then I have to get over 30 sets of training kit laid out for the professional staff, manager and coaches, and the YTS lads. The shirts and shorts have to do them for a week, the socks are clean every day. Friday is the big day as far as the kit is concerned. All the dirty stuff from training has to be carted off to the laundry – then I have to organise playing gear for the following day's youth- and first-team matches."

The move from Eastville to Bath City for home matches has increased the workload on Kendall and match days have to be planned like a military operation.

"I don't think people begin to realise the size of the task. It is enormous, for we take over a thousand items with us," he reveals. "I am often asked if it means that every game is an away game. In fact it is worse than that, for you don't have to carry things like teacups, teapots and toilet-rolls to an away match. That sort of thing is all provided by the home club and those lucky enough to have their own ground will have them on the premises anyway.

"We are not in that fortunate position. We have to keep all our stuff in Portakabins at the bottom of a field at the training ground, move it all out on the morning of a match – and back again afterwards. Can you imagine how long that takes? Let's just say that if I work anything less than 12 hours on a match day I am very lucky.

72

David Mehew is strongly challenged by a Bolton defender.

"We have to do our own catering for supporters at Bath's Twerton Park ground. That means we must have four or five hundred cups and half a dozen teapots. Toilet-rolls are needed for the Board Room, dressing-rooms and spectators – for we have absolutely nothing provided for us at that ground.

"I used to have to cart all this over from Keynsham in an old W-registration Ford Transit Van that was falling apart with rust. Although the terrible state of it was a standing joke among those who did not have to drive it, it was all we could afford at the time. Even so, I was not too happy at getting behind the wheel and often used my own car, a Volvo hatchback. It meant making two trips with stuff piled to the roof. But it was worth it, for I felt safer.

"Fortunately we were able to get rid of that heap of rust when we sold Nigel Martyn (to Crystal Palace) and Gary Penrice (to Watford) last November. Part of the money we received from them went on a Suzuki van, which, at only three years old, was positively brand-new by comparison. And the money we made from the run to Wembley has enabled the club to buy two big kit-hampers – which are a godsend to me. At £400 a time they were out of the question before – how can you even think about buying items like that when the very existence of the club is threatened? But now the position has thankfully eased, the club have bought the hampers, which means I do not have to rely on kitbags any more. They say that every little helps and this should make life a little easier in future.

"But it won't affect my Saturday routine for home matches. I will still leave my house before noon for the drive to Twerton Park and pick up Vi Harris on the way. She is the lovely lady who is Bristol Rovers through and through and does her bit by helping me in the Board Room, making the tea and looking after guests. When we were at Eastville we used to do the buffet as well. But that is now looked after by Joan Dunford, wife of chairman Denis, and Anne Craig, whose husband Ron is a director. They provide a valuable service by bringing in the sandwiches, sausage rolls and the like. And that emphasises the great family spirit at the club. Where else would you find the wives of chairman and directors helping out like that? It is the sort of thing that makes Rovers special and is the reason they survived the financial crisis.

"After I have laid the kit out for the players and made sure all the necessary items have been provided for the visiting team and match officials, I then change into collar and tie to take over my duties as Board Room steward. I set up a bar, look after people as they arrive and make sure they have a drink, cup of tea or whatever at half-time and full-time. When the last person has left the Board Room – and that can be anything up to two hours after the match – I then have to think about moving all the dirty kit, towels, teapots and everything else back to the training ground.

"The luggage even includes a clock! We decided to get hold of one and put it in a prominent place in the dressing-room because we got fed up with players asking us the time. They become edgy as kick-off time approaches and prowl around restlessly, forever asking

'What's the time?' So we got the clock for that reason and take it with us wherever we go.

"Looking after the players' pre-match meal require-ments for away matches and doing the travel arrangements are two of the other jobs that are down to me. The travel at most clubs is done by the secretary and his office-staff. But because we are spread out all over the place that is impossible for Rovers. The ground is at Bath, the training ground at Keynsham and the offices at Two Mile Hill. That means there is not the usual communication and the travel arrangements are left to Roy Dolling and myself. We decide where we stay, what time we leave and where we make a lunch stop when an overnight hotel is not necessary."

A chance meeting at a cricket match began Ray Kendall's long love affair with Bristol Rovers and, as the old song says, "We've been together now for 40 years, and it don't seem a day too much."

"I have loved every minute of it and would not change a thing," says the veteran whose contribution to Rovers has been priceless. "It all started when I went to watch Gloucestershire play Somerset in a county cricket match at Bristol. I met Ron Moules, then assistant secretary at Bristol Rovers, and we got chatting. When he realised how keen I was on football he asked me if I would consider helping out on a part-time basis, as a match-day steward, and it all took off from there.

"I did that and a variety of other jobs for 28 years and moved here full-time when I left the cigarette factory in 1978. Rovers' chairman at the time, Douglas Mearns-Milne, claimed that all the years of voluntary service I had given deserved a full-time job and insisted that I joined the staff here. That was an offer I jumped at.

"I have loved every minute of it and have a fund of wonderful memories that will never leave me. And of all the marvellous things that have happened the best of the lot came in May 1990 – when we won the championship and went to Wembley. In view of everything that had to be overcome by Gerry Francis, his players, the coaching staff and backroom staff, that has to be rated the finest achievement in my 40 years here."

11

Gary Mabbutt

G ARY MABBUTT, Bristol Rovers' most famous footballing son, suffered the heartbreak of missing their final game of a momentous season – the Leyland-Daf Cup final against Tranmere Rovers at Wembley. He was needed in Manchester on Professional Footballers Association business that day and could not get out of it. That was a bitter blow to Mabbutt, who left Eastville in 1982 and went on to find fame and fortune with Tottenham Hotspur and England.

"I was desperately disappointed at having to miss out on Rovers' big day – but there was nothing I could possibly do about it," recalls Mabbutt. "I asked PFA chief Gordon Taylor if it would be possible to give the meeting a miss. But he emphasised the fact that it was a very important one and said as a member of the committee I should be there. I take those union responsibilities very seriously, so there was no question of going against the wishes of Gordon. However, I was there with them in spirit at Wembley, kept as up-to-date as possible on the progress of the game and was very disappointed when I heard they had lost 2-1.

"Even so, Rovers can look back on a wonderful season. Winning the championship has got to be the top target for every club and for the boys to do that and return to the Second Division after all they have been through is a fantastic achievement. A club that was expected to be dead

Gary Mabbutt leads out Tottenham on his return to Eastville in 1983.

The man they call Bruno is beaten by the punch.

and buried a long time ago is now alive and kicking and no one follows their fortunes with closer interest than me.

"I was with the club for five years, as apprentice then full professional, and won 11 Youth and three Under-21 caps for England during that time. That is not bad going, considering they were not one of football's glamour-clubs.

"I am absolutely delighted at the way things have changed for the better for the club I grew up with, for I was born in Bristol and my father, Ray, played for the club for many years. I still go back there a lot, because the family still live there. I spent some time there this summer and could see the joy Rovers' success had brought to their supporters. It's lovely they should have something positive to talk about, instead of constantly discussing the club's survival chances. The pride is back among their fans now."

Mabbutt left Eastville in 1982, in a £105,000 move to Tottenham. That was a bargain price for such a talented, versatile player. But even back in those days Rovers were desperate for money and were ready to snap the hand off anyone who offered it to them. The transfer also placated manager Bobby Gould, furious a couple of months earlier, when Mabbutt had turned down a move to Luton Town.

"Bobby was not happy about that and made it perfectly clear to me he was not pleased. But I could not agree personal terms with David Pleat, the Luton manager at the time and later to be my boss at Spurs. He offered me £50 a week less than I was getting at Bristol Rovers and even though I knew the club were desperate for money to keep them afloat there was no way I could agree to that. After all, I had a mortgage to pay and could not possibly have kept it going on a pay-cut of £50.

"So I was hardly flavour of the month when I turned down a move that had been set up a little while before. Pleat seemed keen to play me at left-back – a position I did not normally occupy in the Rovers team – and asked Gould to play me there for a couple of matches. That was arranged and after Pleat had watched them he then asked Gould to play me in the reserves at Luton. I had not played in the second team for at least four years but readily agreed to do it when Bobby put it to me. That convinced Pleat that I was the man he wanted and the next day he made the offer that Rovers quickly accepted. However when I discovered what he wanted to pay me, that killed the thing stone-dead.

"Rovers got their money and I got my transfer a couple of months later, when Tottenham came in to give me a chance of a move that has turned out very well for me. But Rovers are still very near and dear to my heart. Theirs is still the first result I look for every Saturday and part of me will always belong to them."

12

Geoff Dunford

Director

THERE WAS no prouder man than Geoff Dunford when Bristol Rovers swept to that glorious Third-Division-title success last May. It was the sweetest moment in the life of Dunford, son of chairman Denis, and the man who actually masterminded the plan to save the ailing club from the knacker's yard.

He stood looking in sheer disbelief the night Rovers took neighbours, and bitter rivals, Bristol City apart to clinch promotion back to the Second Division they left in 1981. It was an occasion he never thought he would be able to enjoy and his first thoughts were for the army of volunteers who had made enormous sacrifices to keep the club alive.

"I was a very, very proud man the night we beat City to make sure of promotion. That was a marvellous occasion for everyone who had worked so hard to help us out of a crisis," says Dunford junior. "It was that willingness of so many people to help out, to give valuable time and effort for no reward that helped this club survive when all seemed lost. We will always be grateful for the part these wonderful fans played and let's hope the championship and a day out at Wembley in the Leyland-Daf Cup final was the reward for them. That's the least they deserve for all they did for us."

Dunford was in a parked car, in a lay-by on a busy road on the outskirts of Bristol, when he decided to take on the awesome task of saving a club facing massive financial problems.

"Crazy would be a better word to describe it," he says. "I still don't know why I did it and can assure you I would never attempt anything like this again.

"In October 1985, when the position was probably at its worst – and that is saying something – I was approached by Martin Flook and Barry Bradshaw, Rovers' joint chairmen at the time, and asked if I wanted to buy Flook's 50 per cent shareholding in the club. I said no because I was not the slightest bit interested in getting involved with Bristol Rovers, or so I thought at the time. Roy Redman, now the vice-chairman here, had also been approached soon after me and had been sounded out about joining the Board. So we got together and it was in his car in that lay-by that we decided to take on the massive job of trying to sort Rovers out.

"Flook had by now been back, offering the shares at a very low price because he wanted to get out. But we insisted on getting Bradshaw's shares as well to give us complete control and the power to bring in a completely new Board.

"My father was the obvious choice for chairman as he had retired from the company dairy business and had the time to attend the many meetings that were going on all over the place in an attempt to save the club.

"During the darkest days we were holding three or four Board meetings a week and they lasted anything up to five hours. That gives you some idea of the seriousness of the situation.

"The sale of the training ground at Hambrook – described elsewhere in this book by my father – was the real salvation. That gave us the money to pay off pressing debts and enabled us to keep the Receivers out. And the move to Bath City for home matches was just the thing we wanted. If they had not appeared on the scene to offer help I dread to think what might have happened. We had to leave Eastville, everyone knew that, for our relations with the owners had reached rock bottom – like a man and a wife just before they get divorced. As tenants – and not very welcome ones at that – we were powerless. Our hands were tied and although the place was falling down around us we could do nothing about

Andy Dornan and Devon White adopt a ballet pose!

it. Lots of petty problems were also brought to the surface to make life there very unbearable indeed.

"To make things even more difficult, people whose services we valued very highly walked out because they had had enough and could see no future for Bristol Rovers. Alfred Hill, our highly respected part-time secretary, resigned, insisting the club was insolvent. Chief Executive Gordon Bennett went as well, leaving us new boys all alone and holding the baby.

"The baby somehow survived. But bringing it up was a nightmare experience, one I will never go through again. The many hands offering to help nurse it were invaluable. Without them it would never have survived. So it was great to watch the joy on their faces at the end of a truly wonderful season and to realise that all the effort had been worth while."

13

Bobby Gould

Ex-Manager

B OBBY GOULD is as delighted as every other Bristol Rovers lover
at the phenomenal success achieved by the club last season
and the dramatic revival in its fortunes. But, unlike most others,
Gould is not unduly surprised about it. He always thought the little
club with a massive heart would manage to fight its way back.

Gould had two spells as manager of Rovers – from 1981 to 1983,
then from 1985 to 1987. And he fell in love with the place so much
he kept his house in the city and spent the summer there after falling
out with Wimbledon, his present club where he is on "extended leave"
after a dispute over his contract. "That has given me time to get back
home, catch up on five years' domestic work and listen to all the chat
about Rovers, a very special kind of club," says Gould.

Bobby served a staggering 15 clubs as player, coach and manager
and admits he has fond memories of all of them. But Bristol Rovers is
the one nearest and dearest to his heart. That's why the Midlands-born
Gould decided to keep his home here. He followed their fortunes
closely during a super season and was at Wembley to watch them
play Tranmere in the Leyland-Daf Cup final in May.

"I would have gone anyway, for nothing could have kept me
away from probably the greatest glamour game in the club's
history. But as an added bonus I was asked to do some radio
work.

"I was bitterly upset when they lost to Tranmere, as all
the players were at the time. But once the hurt wore off I
knew they would all look back on a gloriously successful
season. Promotion to the Second Division was the main

aim and they achieved that in some style. To pull that off was absolutely incredible and I don't think too many people know what they had to go through to make it possible.

"People who have spent all their life at the top of the football tree talk about doing away with the Third and Fourth Divisions, claiming they are a liability. In my opinion they are the lifeblood of the game and if you do away with them the game as we know it would die. It is down there at that level you come across the real soccer lover, people who will do anything to keep their club alive.

"There was more pride and passion among Rovers' following than any other club I have been with. Everyone had a fanatical desire to make sure the club never went out of business. And there can't be many other clubs where so many people were willing to rally round and give their time, as they did at Rovers. Some of the characters who sweated to do their bit to keep the bailiffs out were brilliant, people I will never forget.

"Ray Kendall is one. He has been with Rovers for 40 years and still turns his hand to anything that is needed. He is the man who supervises the match-day 'move' to Bath City's Twerton Park ground – and what a move it is. Everything has to be transported from the Cadbury's training ground at Keynsham to Bath. That ranges from playing gear to toilet-rolls! It really is an enormous task, yet Ray cheerfully does that . . . and anything else that needs doing. He also organised the meals on the coach for the journey home from away games in my days at the club. He would pre-cook them at home beforehand, then microwave them on the bus to make sure that a Third Division team without two halfpennies to rub together dined like prosperous First Division giants.

"And there was another diamond in Gertie Grinham, the marvellous lady who took on the job of washing the kit. She would have filthy, muddy gear dumped on her after training and have her machine going all evening so the lads could have it clean and fresh again the next morning.

"It was people like this who kept the Rovers alive, and they will never ever get the financial rewards their efforts

Bobby Gould.

deserve. The lovely thing is that they did not look for money, or other material gain. They did it out of sheer genuine love for the club. And there were hundreds more who did their bit in those times of trouble. We formed a Helpline, where fans paid £2 a week and every Monday they would come to the training ground at Hambrook to watch a video of the previous Saturday's game and question me about it.

"We once had a tremendous victory over Leicester City, beating them 3-1 in the FA Cup. And what a sensation that caused. It was more than standing-room only at the Monday video session after that one. The place was packed to the rafters and fans locked out were clambering up the windows trying to get a glimpse of what was going on inside.

"These people kept the Rovers going when all seemed lost and the intervention of the Dunfords – chairman Denis and his son Geoff – has completed the recovery. What they took over was a mess, a complete and utter shambles. Yet with savage pruning and sensible, businesslike methods, they pulled things round. They took the job on with their eyes wide open, fully aware of the financial mess Rovers were in. Yet there must have been times when even they wondered what they had let themselves in for.

"During my second spell at Rovers – the move from Eastville to Bath took place in that time – the purge had begun and we could not afford a proper staff of full-time professionals. So I had to get by with several non-contract players. I vividly remember going to Lincoln for a Third Division match with only eight players, for non-contract players Gary Smart, Mike England and Phil Purnell – now a full-time pro at Rovers – could not get time off from their jobs to travel with the main party. So I sent the rest on ahead and waited for the other three to finish their day's work before driving them up there. And it illustrated the spirit in the place that we survived all that to earn a 2-2 draw.

"But we were not so lucky at Bournemouth, where again Smart had to follow us on because he was not allowed time off work to travel with us. We got hammered 6-1 on that occasion and the reaction I got from Denis Dunford afterwards made me think I was going mad. Most chairmen would be hopping with fury after a defeat like that. But Mr Dunford turned to me and said, 'Thank you very much for a nice day out.' At first I thought he was being sarcastic. But I suddenly realised he was being serious. It was a marvellous gesture and must go down as one of the most unlikely responses of all time. I can't think of too many chairmen who would say that, and mean it, after getting beaten 6-1.

"The mileage involved after selling the Hambrook training ground and the move to Bath for home matches was phenomenal, for the reserves played their games at Forest Green, so a lot of travelling was involved.

"Through all these troubles the Dunfords somehow managed to keep their sense of humour. One week they had to sell my club car to pay the players' wages – that's how

Carl Saunders shows his threat in front of goal.

bad things were. I had a two-litre Sierra at the time and the money that brought in paid the wages for a week or so. Not long afterwards I asked them about the chances of getting another club car. As they ran a thriving dairy business they told me I could have a milk-float – as long as I did a round on my way to training every morning!

"I did my little bit to keep the Receiver out when the bank were, understandably, putting pressure on and demanding some of their money back . . . or else. I dashed down from Gloucester, where I was at the time, to use a personal friendship and plead with the manager for a bit more time – which, luckily for us, he granted. It was gestures like this that helped the club over a crisis which seemed certain to kill it off, and that proved there was a genuine feeling for the well-being of Bristol Rovers. With attitudes like that and so many willing volunteers ready to give their all there is always a chance. Rovers snatched at that chance . . . but it is still incredible what they have achieved in view of everything they had to overcome. They will always mean something very special to me and I will continue to follow them closely."

14

Gary Penrice

G ARY PENRICE got as much pleasure as anyone else from Rovers' triumphant march back to the Second Division . . . and he was no longer at the club!

Penrice had been sold to Watford for £500,000 last November – a star player sacrificed to ease the crippling financial position. But he is still Rovers through and through and says: "Part of me will always be blue-and-white, the club colours, no matter what I do or I where I go in football."

Penrice, 26, was born in Bristol and played for Mangotsfield – the club that produced among others Phil Purnell, Nicky Tanner, now with Liverpool, Swindon's Steve White and Gary Megson, the much travelled midfield man whose father, Don, once played for and managed Rovers.

"My roots are in the area and I am proud and delighted about what the lads I left behind achieved. It was a fantastic effort, in view of all the problems they have faced," adds Penrice.

"When Nigel Martyn and myself left in November everyone said that Rovers were finished. Pessimists claimed our departure had made the club £1.5 million richer – but killed off any chances of promotion. I never thought that for one second. I always had confidence in the lads' ability to battle on. But deep down I knew the Rovers players were having doubts about the future without two regular members of the side.

"My confidence in them was based on the fact that every setback they had received – and heaven knows there were enough of those – had strengthened their determination to overcome them all. So I was convinced the sale of goalkeeper Nigel to Crystal Palace for £1 million and myself to Watford for half that amount would bring out the best in the rest. And I am absolutely delighted – though by no means surprised to be proved right. Once again the boys showed what they are made of by carrying on as though nothing had happened. They had become so accustomed to getting knocks over the years they simply took the departure of myself and Nigel in their stride.

"In my six years at the club I had seen a lot more 'lows' than 'highs' and Rovers were in so much trouble for so long it would have shocked no one to wake up one morning and find they had gone out of business.

"I started out as an apprentice at neighbours Bristol City, and was there for two years. I was out – along with a lot of others – when they went skint in 1982 and the Receiver was called in. So a shattered 18-year-old thought his dreams of a professional career were in ruins and went to play for non-League Mangotsfield.

"Two years later Rovers made me an offer I was happy to accept, for I was desperate to carve a career in pro football, and I signed in time to play in the last season at Eastville.

"When we moved to Bath, Rovers did not have a penny to call their own. They were broke in a big, big way and some of the things that went on would have opened the eyes of any outsider who thought the world of professional football was a glamorous one. We often used our own cars to get to matches and toured round picking up part-timers from their jobs so they could get to the ground on time.

"The team was never the same two weeks running. It was often a question of whoever was available getting a game. That is what it came down to. I clearly remember we included a young lad from a club called Manor Farm. He played once for us in the Third Division . . . and was never seen again!

"It was a joke situation, a terrible time, and I often wonder

Gary Penrice celebrates.

how the lads got through it. Then Gerry Francis took over as manager and things slowly changed for the better.

"There was no way he could affect what was happening off the pitch – that was beyond his control. But he made all the players believe that anything was possible on it and lifted everyone with his positive approach. That has now paid a rich dividend, with promotion and that Wembley appearance against Tranmere in the Leyland-Daf Cup final.

"I would have loved to have been at Wembley to cheer for the lads on the big day – but I was on tour in Malta with Watford. But my mother, father and grandmother – all Rovers' supporters – were there.

"I don't regret leaving Rovers. I had to do it to better myself. Watford are an ambitious club who wanted a quick return to the First Division. That never worked out last season but it soon will, despite the poor start we have made – a start I missed through injury.

"With 24 goals in each of the previous two summers I am happy with my contribution to the Bristol Rovers' revival. I am delighted they have finished the job I helped to start. And I am particularly pleased for Ian Holloway, another Bristol boy and a great mate of mine. It was a sweet moment for him after living thought the nightmare of knowing his wife had cancer. Happily, she has made a full recovery.

"It is a reward for everyone at the club, for all the hard work they have put in and for all the perseverance and faith they showed through dark, lonely days, when the club's very existence was threatened."

15

Ian Holloway

NO ONE had more cause to celebrate Rovers' marvellous championship success than 27-year-old midfield man Ian Holloway. Only a few short years ago he was being torn apart by personal problems and feared he was all washed-up as a professional footballer.

The local-born Holloway, who joined his beloved Bristol Rovers when barely out of short pants, was struck down with glandular fever – a savage blow to a fit, healthy young athlete. And if that was not enough his girlfriend at the time – now his wife – learned she had a form of cancer.

Hammer-blows like that are devastating enough to rip the heart out of anyone and there were times when Holloway felt like throwing himself off the Clifton Suspension Bridge. But he battled bravely on, overcame his own problem after two long years – then got the joyous news that wife Kim had completely recovered from the cancer. They now have three bonny children – son William, and twin girls Chloe and Eve.

"In view of all that happened it really is a miracle story and we are finding it difficult to believe," says the man who was born and raised in Kingswood. "A couple of years ago life was a complete misery for us. Now it has changed and everything is an absolute pleasure. I think it is fair to say I have had more than my share of setbacks. But winning the Third Division title with Rovers – and pushing neighbours City into second place – makes it all worth while. What a pity we could not have completed the 'double' by beating

Tranmere in the Leyland-Daf Cup final at Wembley. But I suppose you can't have everything and I'll settle for that championship medal."

That is a generous philosophy from a man who used to dread waking up in the morning, fearful of what the day ahead held in store for him. He had taken so many kicks in the teeth, suffered so much heartache he used to dread what would happen next.

"That's the way it gets you when you have been put through the experiences I have. It really gets to you, makes you low and depressed."

Thankfully, Ian is able to smile now as life takes on a happy new meaning for the loyal servant – one of the few of the current Rovers squad who actually played at Eastville.

"That's no more than a name to most of the players at the club now. And although it was hardly the greatest ground in the world I will always have good memories of it," he recalls. "It was where I used to go for coaching as a nine-year-old kid, where I learned the basics of my trade. I signed as an apprentice at 16 and became a full pro two years later.

"After four years, and more than 100 games in the first team, Bobby Gould – the manager at the time – moved me out to Wimbledon. And although I played 19 League games in the season the Dons marched into the First Division that was where my problems really began.

"I lost my snap and sparkle, felt sluggish all the time and did not have to be told I was not playing well. It was a real effort to get through a match. It was quite obvious something was wrong – subsequent events were to reveal the full extent of the problem. It was the start of the glandular fever – an illness that actually took five months to diagnose. If I had found out straight away exactly what was wrong my recovery would have been a lot, lot quicker. Wimbledon manager Dave Bassett – now in charge at Sheffield United – did not exactly come out and accuse me of loafing and not pulling my weight. But the man they call 'Harry' is a tough taskmaster and there was little doubt in my mind he thought

I was taking the easy way out and earning my money under false pretences. It hurt to be judged like that, for I knew there was something physically wrong with me. And when the glandular fever was finally diagnosed I am sure a few people had to swallow their opinions of me.

"Anyway, despite playing a big part in the Dons' historic march into the First Division, just nine years after joining the Football League, I was on my way again. My one season at Plough Lane had clearly not convinced Bassett I was worth a second and the next stop for me was Brentford. Things did not get any better there. But it is where I finally got a long overdue break – with Gerry Francis coming in to take me 'back home' to Bristol Rovers.

"I found it difficult to believe when I heard Gerry was watching me, for I would be the first to admit I was hardly setting the game alight with my performance on the pitch. I knew I was playing badly and Gerry confirmed that view by telling me, 'Every time I watch you, you are absolute rubbish.' I snapped back, 'If that is the case why do you want to buy me then?' To which Gerry replied, 'Because I think I can make a player of you.'

"He seemed so sure of that fact he even loaned the hard-up Rovers the £10,000 Brentford were asking for me. And that was an amazing act of faith if ever I saw one. For a manager to dip into his own pocket for the money to buy someone who had not played well for a long time was absolutely incredible. Happily, the way things have worked out means Gerry got his money back. But there were no guarantees he would at the time. For Rovers had their backs to the financial wall and the game, and the city of Bristol, buzzed with rumours that they could fold at any time.

"For Gerry Francis to do that was the greatest tonic I could possibly have had and I have not looked back since rejoining Rovers after two years away. I finally shook off all the debilitating effects of the fever, got massive peace of mind when Kim received a clean bill of health and it suddenly became a joy to be alive again.

"Helping Rovers win the championship was the greatest thing that has ever happened to me in football. And it means

Devon White strikes again in the 4-2 win over Northampton.

so much more to me, being born in Bristol. Down here you are either City or Rovers. I have always been Rovers, and to push our bitter rivals into second place was the icing on the cake of a wonderful season.

"Even so, as a proud 'Bristolian', I am delighted to have them in the Second Division with us next season. I love my city as much as my club and it will bring extra interest to the place. Let's hope that in a few months' time we are both preparing for the First Division – with us leading the way, of course!

"But for the moment I am just going to sit back and enjoy the exploits of the last season. To experience that after fearing I no longer had a future in the game is a marvellous feeling. To be able to talk about it in years to come to kids I never thought I would have is even better. Right now there is not a happier man in the world than Ian Holloway."

16

Devon White

D EVON WHITE, the man they call Bruno, puts the punch in Rovers' attack and weighed in with 13 goals as they charged to the championship.

Devon, a six-foot-three-inch, 14-stone bundle of aggression, the most popular player at the club had to pinch himself hard when the season was over to make sure he was not dreaming. For yet another of the 'cast-offs' snapped up by Gerry Francis from non-League football thought any chance of glory from the game had passed him by.

The 26-year-old, Nottingham-born White was shown the door after trials at Notts County. He had a short spell at Lincoln before drifting into non-League football with Grantham, Arnold and Boston United.

White proved what a bright spark he is by qualifying as an electrician and earning his living from that during the week. Then enter one Gerry Francis – and the picture changed dramatically.

"I never had to think twice when Gerry made his offer. I had always wanted to be a professional footballer – now I was being given the opportunity to do it," says Dynamite Devon. "I did not know that Rovers were in financial trouble – and I did not care. I just wanted to get out and play for them.

"The problems Rovers have had off the field, plus the management of Gerry on it, have forged a great spirit in the camp. Everyone pulls in the same direction and we are all determined to put this little club on the map.

Devon White.

"Winning the Third Division championship is the first honour I have ever gained, and two or three years ago it would have been the last thing I expected. But since coming here and establishing myself in the team it was no great surprise when it happened. It must have been obvious to everyone that there was no better team in the Third Division. We were among the pacemakers all season and lost only five games in a punishing League programme of 46. Any team with a formidable record like that deserve to be champions. It is obviously the highlight of my career so far. And whatever happens in the future it is something I will always cherish."

Devon had another highlight at Wembley in May when he scored Rovers' goal in a 2-1 Leyland-Daf Cup-final defeat by Tranmere. And even the pain of losing could not take the shine off seeing his name up in lights on the scoreboard in the famous old stadium.

The muscular Devon White matches defenders with his power.

That competition also proved Devon has a long memory. For Rovers' victims in the area final were Notts County, the club who decided White was not good enough for them. "After that experience it was a nice feeling to put it across them and clinch our place at Wembley," he smiled.

"My ambition for the future? To be the best at anything I do. That has always been my aim. I may never reach the top – but that won't stop me trying. I am enjoying life at the moment like never before. I just hope this goes on and my electrician's tools are stored in the bag for a long time yet."

You can be sure that Devon will be wired in and ready to hand out a few shocks to Second Division defenders this season.

17

Steve Yates

THEY ARE calling Steve Yates the finest home-grown talent at Rovers since Gary Mabbutt. And you cannot get higher praise than that. Bristol-born Mabbutt, whose father Ray also played for Rovers, while "rebel" brother Kevin was with City, earned England Youth honours in his time at Eastville – remember that? – before moving on to fame and fortune at Tottenham, where he has been skipper for several seasons. So if 20-year-old centre-half Yates does as well in his career as Mabbutt he will have plenty to look back on and be proud of.

And Yates, the quiet man of the club, makes no secret of his desire to play First Division football as soon as possible.

"Of course I want to play in the First Division. Doesn't every player with a scrap of ambition in him?" says the man who still has two years to run on his current contract with the club.

"And of course it's very flattering to be compared with Gary Mabbutt. Everyone in this city knows what a great player he is. He was Rovers through and through – and so am I. I was born in the area and came to the club as a ten-year-old. I also trained with City for a while, but I preferred what this club had to offer so I decided to link up with them.

"I was taken under the wing of Roy Dolling, the club physio and Youth Development Officer. I have worked my way through and have been a first-team regular for the last two years.

Steve Yates.

"It's absolutely brilliant the way things have worked out for me. To have won a Third Division championship medal and appeared in a Wembley cup final at the age of twenty can't be at all bad. It is much better than anything I could have hoped for.

"Although my Mum and Dad are originally from Birmingham they are rabid Rovers followers now. So are all the rest of the family. It was the occasion for a party when we beat Bristol City 3-0 to make sure of promotion to the Second Division. Everyone in the Yates household enjoyed that one.

"I'm known as the quiet man of the club, but I have my say on the field when it's necessary. I do make myself heard when I think the time is right.

"I am delighted to have established myself in the team at such a young age and missed only four games last season. One was through injury, three for suspension – which I think was

Steve Yates is beaten by Goalkeeper David Felgate.

harsh. I was sent off for a foul at Orient. Yet I considered myself hard-done-by, for all I did was a sliding tackle on a greasy, wet pitch. I was not happy to get a red card – but put it down as all part of my football experience. I most definitely learned a lesson from that and intend to keep learning them in the Second Division. That is an adventure I am really looking forward to."

If some managers have their way they will enable Yates to leapfrog the Second Division and take him straight into the First. And that would surprise few of the people who have watched him grow up at Rovers and develop into one of the most talented young men in the game. For Gary Mabbutt read Steve Yates. He is almost certain to be the next to hit the glory trail – and bring some more welcome money into the bank account.

Ray Kendall, Rovers' kit man who has been involved with the club for 40 years, has no doubts Yates has the footballing world at his feet. Kendall has seen dozens of outstanding players in the famous blue and white quartered shirts in his time with them. He is convinced that none have been better prospects than Yates.

"That kid is a diamond and there is no way we could ever hope to hold on to him. He is destined to go right to the very top" claims Kendall. "Apart from being a very good young player he is also extremely dedicated and is a nice lad. He works hard at his game and never gives a minute's trouble. He is a cert to make a big impression in football and it is only a question of time before one of the glamour clubs make a move for him."

Even though Rovers' need for money is now not so urgent – the championship and Wembley appearance brought a welcome windfall – they still would not stand in Yates's way if a top club came in. The kid has the ambition to go with his talent and Gerry Francis would do nothing to block the career of one of the most outstanding youngsters ever produced in the West Country. So Rovers supporters had better enjoy Yates while they have still got him. The way things are going that will not be long.

18

Carl Saunders

F BRISTOL ROVERS had their way they would take Carl Saunders to a
security vault after training each day and lock him away for the
night! That way they could sleep easily themselves, knowing no
harm could come to their most expensive asset. For Carl cost £70,000
from Stoke City last February and that represents untold riches for a
club in Rovers' sticky financial situation.

Saunders is by far the most expensive player on the club's books.
In fact Ian Holloway – bought with £10,000 manager Gerry Francis
loaned the club himself – was the only other one to cost a fee until
Gerry paid another £10,000 for Tony Pounder from non-League
Weymouth in July.

In view of the problems Rovers faced, it was an enormous gamble
for them to cough up the money Francis wanted to buy a full-back
languishing in Stoke's reserve team. But cough up they did – and they
have reaped a handsome dividend on their outlay. Francis moved
Saunders into a striker's role and his goals shot them to promotion
and the Leyland-Daf Cup final against Tranmere Rovers.

Rovers, of course, lost that 2-1 at Wembley. But Saunders and
his team-mates are adamant it would have been a different story
if they had been awarded a penalty when Carl, having broken
clean through, was pole-axed by Tranmere 'keeper Eric Nixon.
Referee Vic Callow amazed even the Tranmere supporters in the
stadium by waving play on. That decision incensed Rovers, and
Saunders will insist to his dying day the referee dropped a king-sized
clanger.

The move to Rovers transformed the career of the 25-year-old
Birmingham-born Saunders, who seemed to be going nowhere fast
until Francis stepped in to offer him a fresh start. And Carl had a
lot to live up to, for he was signed to replace golden-boy striker

Carl Saunders.

Gary Penrice, sold to Watford for £500,000 two months later. It was a challenge he took on manfully and responded to magnificently. In fact he did the job so well that Penrice, local-born hero of the Rovers fans, was hardly missed as the promotion spot was clinched.

"To have any chance of making an impression you have got to have an incentive, a target to aim at. And there was not too much incentive for me in the reserves at Stoke," says the bubbly Saunders. "So coming here was the best thing that ever happened to me. It really gave my career a boost by providing something to play for. Taking over from Penrice did not bother me for one moment. I just wanted to show what I could do and Rovers were offering me the chance to do it.

"The spirit among the lads at Rovers is tremendous. But

Carl Saunders turns on the style with an overhead kick.

then you expect it to be like that when things are going well. There is nothing like a bit of success to get things buzzing inside any football club. And I intend to enjoy every minute of it, for I have had far too much of the other side of footballing life and know only too well what it is like to struggle.

"I know one or two other clubs were interested when Stoke were ready to let me go. I believe Notts County wanted me on loan. But Gerry Francis wanted me on a permanent basis and that was good enough for me. If I needed any convincing, that was the thing that clinched it for me and things have gone like a dream since I came here.

"After playing so long at full-back I suppose I was a bit surprised when Gerry said he wanted to play me up front. But he's the guv'nor and I was happy to fall in with whatever he wanted. And I don't think it worked out too badly, for in my few months here I finished with eight goals. As that helped us to the prize of promotion I suppose that means everyone was satisfied.

"The scenes that followed our 3-0 win over Bristol City at Twerton Park to clinch promotion were quite amazing. I had never experienced anything like them in all my life. It brought home to me just how much this club means to the people who have followed it through thick and thin. To make sure of promotion by putting one across the local rivals really gave those fans something to savour. It was a pleasure to be part of it and I hope we can give those supporters much more to cheer about in the next couple of years.

"I have had my share of ups and downs since I turned pro with Stoke at 18 – and there were too many 'downs' for my liking. Now life is suddenly looking a whole lot better and I intend to make the most of the golden opportunity I have been given."

19

Paul Nixon

P AUL NIXON is another who wondered if he had a future at Rovers after a clash with manager Gerry Francis. They had such a violent set-to that the police were called and both Nixon and Francis were taken for questioning.

It all blew up when Nixon — a Geordie who emigrated to New Zealand and won six international caps for that country — discovered he had been dropped for the match against Brentford last season. He reacted angrily to the news, then confronted Francis about it again afterwards. That's when the sparks flew and the long arm of the law stretched out to part the warring factions.

"I must admit I got very upset when Gerry told me I was out, for I did not think I deserved to be," recalls Nixon. "It would be accurate to say that things between us got very heated and a few eyebrows were raised at the intensity of our argument. It was a lot more serious than the normal run-of-the-mill rows you get at football clubs and I genuinely feared that I had put my future at the club in doubt.

"Both Gerry and I were big enough to accept our share of the blame for what had happened and after a lot of soul-searching I decided to stay and fight to establish myself again. However, despite assurances that I *was* wanted here I found myself completely out in the cold for two months. I found that too much to take — so went in and asked for a transfer. Although Gerry said he did not want me to go he

Paul Nixon.

agreed to make me available and promised to let me know if anyone came in for me. But the March deadline passed and nobody did, so Gerry asked me to come off the list. There was no point in sticking out as an act of defiance at that stage, so I agreed to his request. He showed he does not bear grudges by involving me again fully with the team. We now get on so well no one would ever know our bust-up happened and peace between us has been restored. I am now more happy to stay with this club, battle for a place and help them to more success in the future years."

Nixon, who joined Rovers in January 1989, showed what he is

capable of with a fine display after coming on as substitute in the Leyland-Daf Cup final against Tranmere at Wembley. He replaced the unfortunate Ian Alexander — carried off with an injury — and turned in a game that made him a prime candidate to be nominated Rovers' man-of-the-match.

That put the finishing touch to a season in which this useful all-round player scored six goals in 28 games and he will obviously figure prominently in the Francis plans as Rovers tackle Second Division football.

20

Andy Reece

TELL MIDFIELD-MAN Andy Reece he had a good year as Bristol Rovers won promotion and a Wembley date and you will get a wry smile from him. For Good Year – the tyre factory in the industrial Midlands – was where 27-year-old Reece earned his living before Gerry Francis offered him a career in football. It was yet another master stroke by the wheeler-dealer Francis, who has moulded a collection of misfits into a formidable team. Reece, from Willenhall and a lifelong Wolves fan, jumped eagerly at the chance and is now one of Rovers' most influential players.

"Like most kids I dreamed of being a professional footballer. But clubs were not exactly falling over themselves to sign me and I thought there was no chance of it happening," he said. "I was an apprentice at Walsall, but when they decided I was not good enough to keep on their staff I knew I had to look for another way to earn a living. So I got a job working shifts in the Good Year tyre factory. I did not like it, but there was not a lot I could do about it.

"I was playing for a Sunday morning team in the West Midlands at the time. The manager knew Kenny Hibbitt – who has recently left Rovers to take over at Walsall – and asked him to come and watch me play. We won the match Kenny was at 4-1 and I scored two of the goals. I must have done enough to impress, for I was invited down to Bristol and had two games in the reserves when Bobby

Gould was manager. Then Bobby left and Gerry Francis took over. He asked me to come down for a trial – and it was not really a great hardship to take time off from Good Year to do it.

"After two weeks here I was offered a pro-contract and was on my way to achieving a boyhood dream. What has happened since has been like a fairy story. To come from Sunday morning parks football and a job making tyre treads to a Third Division championship medal and an appearance at Wembley is real *Roy of the Rovers* stuff.

"In my case it is joy of the Rovers, for you would have to go a long way to find a happier, more contented young man than me. It has gone brilliantly in my three seasons here. In fact I often have to ask myself if all this is really happening to me. I am really grateful to Gerry for giving me my big chance and would like to think I have gone some way to repaying the faith he showed in me.

Andy Reece heads on to the crossbar.

"Beating neighbours Bristol City to clinch promotion, then winning at Blackpool to make sure of the title in front of more than 5,000 of our fans produced scenes I will never forget as long as I live. The reaction to that was quite incredible and I felt so pleased for all the people who have stuck loyally by us through all our problems.

"A particularly enjoyable occasion for me was going to Molineux, famous home of the Wolves I had supported as a kid, and beating them 1-0. I took a lot of pleasure out of that result, I can assure you. That has to rate as my own personal highlight of any season. But that was in the Third Division towards the end of the 1988/9 campaign. Now this term we play Wolves in the Second Division. And you don't need me to tell you how much I am looking forward to that.

"In fact I look forward to everything about my life these days. To be paid for doing something I love makes me a very privileged young man and I would not swop places with anyone. When you started out the way I did you have to think yourself lucky to get a dream chance. It is a million times better than working in that tyre factory.

"My ambitions for the future? To do well in the Second Division and be happy. I would willingly settle for that."

21

Tony Sealy

Tony Sealy felt like an uninvited guest at a wedding as Rovers put the finishing touches to their marvellous season. For the much-travelled, 31-year-old Londoner was forced to sit out the last month of the season after breaking his right leg in a match against Cardiff at Twerton Park. But missing the vital run-in, as Rovers clinched the Third Division championship and a place in the Leyland-Daf Cup final at Wembley, caused him much more pain than the hairline fracture that put him out of action.

"It was heartbreaking to be forced to sit on the sidelines and watch it all happening for the lads. No words can ever describe how badly I felt about it," said Sealy, Rovers' most experienced player and one who will be vital to their Second Division campaign.

"I did the damage – which was the same injury Crystal Palace striker Ian Wright had – in the game against Cardiff. But I was not as lucky as him, for he recovered in time to appear at Wembley in the FA Cup final. Mine cost me my place in Rovers' team for the Leyland-Daf final against Tranmere and vital promotion-clinching games. I missed the last month of the season after being almost an ever-present before the injury.

"It all might have been so different if the extent of the injury had been discovered earlier. In fact I was actually playing with the broken leg. The reason for that is that it was

Tony Sealy.

not diagnosed for some time after I did the damage. X-rays I had in the two weeks immediately afterwards showed nothing. We thought it might be just a heavy knock and I played on hoping things would improve. When they did not I had another X-ray that finally revealed the fracture. That meant I had to have a rest – there was no other choice. And it was a real sickener to miss the most important part of the season, the part where everything the lads had worked so hard for and dreamed about became a reality.

"The only other problem I had during the season was a split head early in the New Year. Carl Saunders was signed during my absence on that occasion, started scoring goals straight away and it took me three weeks to get back in the team.

Tony Sealy shoots for goal.

"I know that injuries are part and parcel of the game and that as a professional footballer you have got to accept them. But this last one was very costly, depriving me of a Wembley appearance. I made one with Southampton in the 1979 League Cup final and at the age of 31 will not have too many more chances of going there. But overall I have been very lucky and don't suppose I can really complain about the way the game has treated me."

Sealy has played for Crystal Palace, Queen's Park Rangers, Fulham, Leicester, Bournemouth, Sporting Lisbon and was a non-contract player with Brentford when Gerry Francis signed him for Rovers in September 1989.

"This is the fifth championship side I have been involved with, and that's a record to be proud of. Palace, Rangers, Bournemouth and Sporting Lisbon all won titles while I was with them. That makes this latest one all the more disappointing. It would have been nice to go all the way and finish the job off, instead of being forced out like that. But I will just have to make up for it by helping Rovers to do well in the Second Division.

"I know I can go on for a long time yet. After more than 300 games in the Football League and in Europe my condition is as good as it ever was. They are obsessed with fitness in Portugal and run health checks on players all the time. The last one I had before I left confirmed I have the heart and lungs of a 26-year-old. So there is a lot of mileage in me yet and I am really looking forward to the Second Division with Rovers.

"Obviously it was a big gamble for me to come here. The set-up is vastly different to Sporting Lisbon – one of the biggest clubs in the world. And their financial situation is also somewhat different to Rovers . . . they have got lots of money, for a start. But you don't have to spend long at this club to smell success. You can sense what is going on and I am convinced the future is rosy for Rovers.

"I have known Gerry for years, from our days as players together at Palace and QPR. He is a winner and I love men with attitudes like that. He has most definitely got things right here. Under Gerry Francis, Rovers are going places . . . and I want to make the journey with them.

"For a lot of the boys at this lovely little club, going into the Second Division will be a journey into the unknown. But they will enjoy it and do themselves, and Bristol Rovers, proud."

22

Christian McLean

C HRISTIAN MCLEAN has kept Gerry Francis busy, turning down transfer requests that have been slapped in. The six-foot-four-inch, 14-stone powerhouse is unhappy at failing to command a regular place in the team and wants the chance to prove himself elsewhere.

The 26-year-old, who used to work for a record pressing company, and played non-League football with Clacton and Chelmsford, has the unenviable task of trying to get Devon White's place in the team. And the immensely popular White – the man they call "Bruno" – has delivered a knockout blow to McLean's hopes of a regular first-team spot.

Christian joined Rovers two-and-a-half years ago and last season scored four goals in his nine appearances. He is yet another of the players discovered in soccer's backwoods by Francis – who rates McLean so highly he is refusing to let him go.

"Every time I have made a transfer request the manager has told me I must stay. I asked him for a move three times and each time the answer was 'No'," says McLean.

"He turned me into a striker after bringing me here. I feel I have done well every time I have been in the team – that's why I am so upset at not getting more of a chance to prove myself. I don't believe I have deserved to be dropped. I find myself battling big Devon for the place up front – and it's a battle it seems I just cannot win. But every time I ask the manager for a transfer he tells me I am part of his

Christian McLean enjoys some rare first-team action.

Christian McLean.

plans and must stay. Even so I am still not happy with the situation and would go if it meant getting first-team football somewhere else."

23

Phil Purnell

PHIL PURNELL spent a happy summer basking in the glory of winning a Third Division championship medal with Bristol Rovers and appearing in their showpiece Leyland-Daf Cup final against Tranmere Rovers. And surely few would begrudge that glow of self-contentment to a 25-year-old midfield man who thought his career was over before it had even got started.

Purnell, local-born and one of only three of the current squad – skipper Vaughan Jones and Ian Holloway are the others to have played at Eastville, has been plagued by injury since the tender age of eight! He was out of the game completely for two years – from 16 to 18 – and admits there were times he feared he would never play again. "That was a distinct possibility after all the problems with injury I had suffered," recalls Purnell, now happily fighting fit.

"I joined Rovers as a schoolboy when I was 11 and spent the next five years with the club. Then a pelvic injury flared-up and forced me to stop playing for two years. I broke a leg twice as an eight-year-old kid and medical men suspect that led to the later pelvic problem. That was just a theory. What was hard fact was that I was forced to quit playing football for two long years. That was a heartbreaking time for me.

"Like most football-mad lads I had always dreamed of becoming a professional and after this setback I saw my chances of doing it going up in smoke. I was devastated but had to start planning for the future, so I took a three-year

124

Phil Purnell at full stretch.

apprenticeship with British Aerospace here in Bristol. When that ended I went to work with my father selling furniture and trying to make some sort of football career for myself.

"I had recovered from my pelvic injury and started playing again with top local side Mangotsfield – the club that produced Gary Penrice, Gary Megson and Liverpool defender Nicky Tanner among many others. Thankfully things started to go right for me at long last and I was given a part-time contract by Rovers. I was still working with my Dad and was one of the players the rest used to pick up as they toured the area before matches. There was none of the luxury of meeting a coach. We could not afford that in those days and players often used their own cars and acted as taxi-drivers.

"I did well enough to earn a full contract to achieve my boyhood dream and made my first-team début against Bristol City on New Year's Day 1986. The fact that the opposition was provided by the city's 'other' team, our deadly rivals, means I will never forget that anyway. But the game sticks in my mind for another reason – Gerry

Phil Purnell celebrates Rovers' goal at Wembley in the Leyland-Daf Cup final.

Francis, now our manager, was playing for us in those days and was stretchered off with a bad injury.

"Gerry has worked wonders to revive a club in grave danger of folding up and what has happened here in the past couple of years has been little short of a miracle. For Rovers to revive the way they have after losing their ground, training ground and almost everything else, is wonderful anyway. For me to have a part in it after fearing I would never play again is absolutely fantastic."

If Purnell thought it would all be plain sailing after getting his cherished full-time contract with the club he had followed all his life, he was in for a rude shock. For the injury hoodoo struck yet again before the season started.

"I had an operation last August after damaging ligaments and cartilage in my right knee and missed the first half of last season," said Purnell. "It was January before I was back in action again, so I had a lot of catching up to do. Fortunately I managed to do it and play a part in a campaign that provided memories to last me a lifetime.

"The highlight was unquestionably beating neighbours City 3-0 at Twerton Park to clinch promotion to the Second Division. It is always nice to put it across City. To do it with so much at stake – such a big prize at the end of it – was an extra bonus. And it was also a marvellous feeling when we drew 0-0 at Notts County in the Leyland-Daf Cup – after winning the first leg 1-0 – to realise we were at Wembley. That was the icing on the cake as far as I was concerned and at that moment all the injury heartbreak I had suffered was forgotten. It was worth all that to be part of last season's achievements and I hope I can take it on from here."

24

Bob Twyford

Secretary

THE PHRASE "glutton for punishment" must have been invented for people like Bob Twyford. For after serving time as secretary of Bristol City Football Club – an outfit which went broke and had to re-form after running into terrible financial problems – he then took on the same job with Bristol Rovers. As everyone now knows, Rovers have lived on a knife-edge for years and it seemed that Twyford, a 52-year-old former policeman, was jumping out of the frying pan into the fire.

"I knew all about the problems Rovers had and when I took the job on here I admit I wondered just how long I would be in work. If I listened to all the pessimists, all the prophets of doom, the club was set to collapse at any minute," says Twyford.

"I had a long chat with Gordon Bennett, the former Chief Executive here, before I accepted the job. And what he told me gave me encouragement and suggested there was hope for Rovers.

"After two fine seasons, culminating in winning the Third Division championship and going to Wembley in the Leyland-Daf Cup final, things are going well and we are in the black at last. Bristol Rovers are now doing something they have not done for a very long time . . . making money. So I am delighted at the way things have worked out and it has proved to be a very good move for me.

128

Bob Twyford.

"But even before we turned the corner and put the bulk of our troubles behind us I still considered myself fortunate to have got this job. I was not the Rovers' first choice. Someone else was offered the job ahead of me, but he turned it down. Rovers then came back to me and I jumped at the chance to get back into full-time football. Opportunity does not often knock twice. It did for me and I am very grateful for that."

That was a dramatic about turn by Twyford, an ex-police-sergeant, who was a Press and Public Relations Officer during his time in the force. For when he walked out on Bristol City five years ago after an outbreak of violence among Ashton Gate followers, he vowed never to go back into the game. The man who had spent his working life trying to enforce and uphold the law had been sickened by the antics of the hooligan element, who have for too long disfigured our national game and caused our clubs to be treated as the lepers of Europe.

"Hooliganism was at its peak then and there was some trouble when City played at Reading. Terry Cooper, the manager at the time, threatened to resign and I was in the mood to go with him. Then we played Millwall at Ashton Gate and the scenes of violence there were horrifying. I had been in the police-force all my life and never thought I would see the day when officers in full riot gear were needed at a football match. But it happened on this occasion – and that was enough for me. I could not stomach things like that and wanted no part of it. I have never been so upset by anything in my life and I knew I had to get out.

"I also had a problem with my health – happily cleared up now – that reinforced my decision to quit. And at that time it was the end of it as far as I was concerned. But football gets in the blood and it was not too long before I was itching to return. So when I heard Rovers – who by now had moved out of Eastville and into Bath's Twerton Park ground, and were being run by a completely new Board of Directors – were looking for a secretary I knew I wanted the job.

"Before I went to City I was told I had to give the job a chance – I had to be there for at least two years before I knew how things would work out. Because of the problems with the fans I did not do that. I quit after only 18 months. That was obviously not long enough and, deep down, walking out was probably wrong – something I should not have done.

"Football has always been in my blood, even though I did not work full-time in it until I went to Ashton Gate. So it was not too long after leaving them I knew I would love to get back into the game. Rovers gave me that chance and I never hesitated about taking the job for one second, even though they were reported to be broke and in danger of folding up at any minute.

"When I came here the new Board were desperately trying to clear off debts of over £400,000 – not an easy thing to do when you have no assets – and wipe out weekly losses of £5,000. If Bath City had not come in and offered us the use of their ground to play our home matches on, I dread to think what would have happened. Without Twerton Park there surely would have been no future for us.

"The average gate when I first went to Rovers was under 3,000. It was not that the fans had rebelled against the move

– that was more or less all the Rovers could pull in in those dark days. Last season the average was 6,200. So the success we have enjoyed on the field has doubled the gates. But the people off the field – the Board and backroom staff – have played their part as well. Rovers are now in the black for the first time in years. And it has taken a lot of hard work by a lot of people to bring about that happy situation.

"The commercial manager, the lottery manager, shop staff, office staff, part-time match-day staff – everyone with Bristol Rovers at heart has worked tirelessly to do their bit for the club. Everyone has pulled together to produce a close-knit family and a lovely atmosphere that makes it a pleasure to work here.

"At a lot of clubs the directors are on a joy-ride, an ego trip. They are in it for the prestige and contribute little in real terms. At Bristol Rovers the directors put a lot in and take very little out. The sensible budgeting they imposed after taking control in 1986 is responsible for bringing this club back from the dead. So all Rovers' supporters owe a huge debt to chairman Denis Dunford and his Board for keeping the Receivers out.

"What has happened here is a fairy tale. For Rovers to have achieved all this against the crippling odds they faced is a truly remarkable story."

25

David Williams

Former Player-Manager

GERRY FRANCIS should have won the Manager of the Year award for his magnificent achievement of leading Bristol Rovers to promotion from the Third Division and to the Leyland-Daf Cup final at Wembley. That's the unshakeable opinion of David Williams, former player-manager at Eastville and now assistant boss and chief coach at First Division Norwich City.

Williams, a Welsh international midfield player and also a qualified schoolteacher, feels it is a travesty of justice that Gerry's remarkable feat did not get wider recognition.

"No one should try to minimise what Gerry has done for Rovers. To get them out of the Third Division and to a showpiece Wembley final on the slender resources he has to work with is a superb achievement," says Williams, "and I think it is a great shame he did not get recognised more for it. You see Kenny Dalglish getting the Manager of Year award again, yet he does not have any of the restrictions placed on him that Gerry had. You see Joe Royle getting a special award for what he did for Oldham – reaching the final of the Littlewoods Cup and semi-final of the FA Cup. Of course Joe did well, and he got some recognition for it. So why not an award for Gerry Francis who in my view did as good a job as any manager in the country last season?

"Although I have been away from Bristol for five years

David Williams.

now I still keep in close contact with the city and the club and have a lot of friends still involved with Rovers. I know what they have had to go through in financial terms, the sacrifices they have had to make. I am full of admiration for the way they have come through it. To have no ground, no training ground and no real facilities to call your own is a demoralising feeling. You are like outcasts, a club no one wants.

"When I played for Rovers we had the Eastville ground and a training centre at Hambrook, which had marvellous facilities. If anything they were better than the ones we have at Norwich City now – and they are envied by a lot of people. We had practice pitches and a floodlit synthetic area that could be let for community use during the week. And that was our base as well. We operated from there and moved into Eastville only for matches. The big problem was that the club did not own Eastville – it was leased from the Stadium Company that did. So even then we felt like outsiders. It did not seem like home and there was a strange feeling. But at least we were a Bristol club, still playing in Bristol. How they coped with leaving Eastville and moving out of the city altogether I just do not know. The training ground had to go to bring in money to keep the club alive and that was another strong link broken. So to survive all that and still win promotion is little short of a miracle.

"I must admit I did not think they would do it. I thought they had done extremely well to make the play-offs the previous season and when they were forced to sell Gary Penrice and Nigel Martyn it seemed inevitable that they had sold their promotion chance with it. However, the problems they were facing forged a tight bond and a wonderful spirit, and that pulled them through.

"The money-worries that everyone knows about now were probably there when I was manager for two years from 1983 to 1985, but I was not aware of them and went about my business believing the club was on a sound financial footing.

"I had been at Rovers since I was a ten-year-old kid, travelling over from Cardiff to train and play for them. I made my début at 20, while still a part-timer at teacher training college and turned full professional at 23.

"Don Megson was the manager when I first got in the team and he was very much a Rovers man, having also played for the club as a full-back. Then Bobby Gould took over and I was club captain when Gould left to take over at Coventry in May 1983.

"Myself and other senior players Aidan McCaffrey, Tim Parkin and Brian Williams were asked by Martin Flook, the chairman at the time, if we wanted the manager's job at Eastville. The other three said 'No'. But management was something I had always fancied having a go at. So, despite the fact I was only 28, I told him I wanted the job.

"It came down to a choice between Alan Ball and myself in the end. The former England World Cup star – who had a marvellous playing career with Blackpool, Everton, Arsenal and Southampton – was also interviewed for the job. But I apparently got it because my long connection with the club meant I could go in with first-hand experience of the place and that I was known by the people there.

"I went for the job knowing I had nothing to lose, for if it all went wrong for me as a manager I was still young enough to go back to being a player.

"In the two seasons I was in charge we finished fifth, then sixth, in the Third Division, so I can look back with some satisfaction on the job I did. But combining the two roles, playing and managing, was difficult. It imposed a strain on me and after a couple of years I was looking for a change, knowing I still had a lot to offer as a player.

"I knew that meant breaking with Bristol Rovers. I had to leave the club, for it would have been impossible to continue there as a player under a new manager. Once it was established I would be leaving, I started to get a few calls. I spoke to Ian Branfoot, then at Reading – then Ken Brown came in with an offer to sign for Norwich.

"Norwich had just won the Milk Cup and were comfortably placed in the First Division when I agreed to sign for them. Then an incredible form slump saw them slide rapidly down the table into a relegation place. So I had agreed to join a First Division club which had actually dropped into the Second Division by the time I started playing for them.

"I still maintain close links with Bristol Rovers and was down there recently playing in a golf day for Vaughan Jones, who is in his Testimonial year. What brilliant timing he showed, choosing a year when Rovers had such a wonderful season.

135

"I am full of admiration for the job everyone there has done. And the club must know they have done very well to hang on to their outstanding young manager. When Gerry took them to the play-offs last season he was in demand and could have moved to a bigger club. After winning the championship and going to Wembley I thought it was a certainty he would move on this time. But it is the sort of club you develop an affinity with and I suppose the fact the fans were desperate to keep him influenced his decision as well.

"Rovers are on the move again after surviving some difficult years and I will follow their progress with close interest."

26

David Mehew

D AVID MEHEW, the man they call 'Boris Becker', served up the goals that sent Bristol Rovers shooting into the Second Division. Mehew earned the nickname because he is a lookalike for the West German tennis-ace, twice a former Wimbledon champion. But Mehew's aim is to put the ball *in* the net, not over it, and the 22-year-old, Reading-born player has succeeded in superb style.

The 21 goals he rattled in from midfield last season got the big clubs sitting up and taking notice and now the First Division predators are at most Rovers matches watching yet another kid who thought he had no future with the club. But he is more than happy to stay with Rovers and try to help the homely West Country outfit into the First Division.

"I see no reason why that should not happen. We proved far and away the best side in the Third and have the organisation and ability to do well in the Second," he says. "If Rovers decide they want to sell me there is not a lot I can do about that, but I won't be pressing to leave for I am happy here now. I am aware there is a lot of speculation about my future. I don't allow that to bother me and I just get on with my game."

Mehew was a raw kid at Rovers when Gerry Francis arrived as manager three years ago, and he immediately assumed he was surplus to requirements.

David Mehew in action.

"When Gerry took over I thought I did not fit in with his plans. Things definitely never went well for me and my belief that my days here were numbered was reinforced when I was sent out on loan to non-League clubs Bath and Trowbridge.

"I was feeling sorry for myself and wondering what the future held, when it slowly dawned on me that I was the one at fault. If I was not making a go of it, it was down to me. It was my attitude that was wrong and if things were not working out here for me then I had no one to blame but myself. That was the bolt of realisation that suddenly hit me. When I sat down and tried to analyse what had gone wrong I realised that for some reason I had been sulking. I don't know what the reason for that was – perhaps it was because I thought I was no longer wanted. Whatever it was I knew I had to snap out of it – and fast. In this game you have to fight to establish yourself and going around full of self-pity will get you nowhere. Fortunately I came to my senses in time and when I was brought back here after

138

David Mehew goes for goal against Notts County.

my spell on loan I grabbed the opportunity that was being presented to me.

"Like most of the other lads here I never for one moment thought all this would happen – that I would be the proud owner of a Third Division championship medal and make an appearance in a glamour Wembley Cup final with more than 30,000 West Country fans cheering us on. As a starry-eyed youngster these are the sort of things you dream about. To actually experience them is fantastic.

"We were all a bit down in the dumps when the club was forced to sell Gary Penrice and Nigel Martyn. Even though we knew it had to be done for the financial well-being of the club it still came as a big blow to us. And when neighbours Bristol City opened up a seven-point gap on us at the top of the table we thought that was it – our chances of winning promotion had been blown.

"But the manager acted in his usual decisive way to replace Gary and Nigel and we slowly got back to our best and closed the gap on City. And when we beat them 3-0 on that marvellous night at Twerton Park to clinch promotion it provided me with the biggest thrill of my life. At that moment I did not think anything could happen to top that.

"I was proved wrong soon afterwards when we won at Blackpool to make sure of finishing as champions. The scenes that accompanied that were simply fantastic. More than 5,000 of our fans had made the journey north to cheer us on and they turned the whole occasion into a carnival. The spectacle they provided, the way they reacted to Rovers' greatest achievement for many years is something I will never forget. For me that was the season's big highlight.

"Hopefully the problems for this club are now over and we can face the future with confidence. I honestly see no reason why we can't do well in the Second Division. Keeping the same group of players together was the secret behind the success and that will probably be the case next season as well.

"Rovers gave me another chance when they could have slung me out over my attitude. I would love to repay them by helping them into the First Division for the first time in their history."

Fixtures – 1989/90

Barclays League Division Three

Date		Opposition	H/A	Res./Sc.	Att.
Sat.	19. 8.89	Brentford	H	W 1-0	5835
Sat.	26. 8.89	Mansfield Town	A	W 1-0	
Sat.	2. 9.89	Notts County	H	W 3-2	4753
Sat.	9. 9.89	Bolton Wanderers	A	L 0-1	
Sat.	16. 9.89	Preston North End	H	W 3-0	4350
Sat.	23. 9.89	Bristol City	A	D 0-0	
Tue.	26. 9.89	Leyton Orient	A	W 1-0	
Sat.	30. 9.89	Reading	H	D 0-0	6120
Sat.	7.10.89	Fulham	H	W 2-0	5811
Sat.	14.10.89	Bury	A	D 0-0	
Tue.	17.10.89	Cardiff City	A	D 1-1	
Sat.	21.10.89	Northampton Town	H	W 4-2	4920
Sat.	28.10.89	Chester City	A	D 0-0	
Wed.	1.11.89	Huddersfield Town	H	D 2-2	6467
Sat.	4.11.89	Blackpool	H	D 1-1	5360
Sat.	11.11.89	Shrewsbury Town	A	W 3-2	
Sat.	25.11.89	Swansea City	H	W 2-0	5623
Sat.	2.12.89	Walsall	A	W 2-1	
Fri.	15.12.89	Crewe Alexandra	A	L 0-1	
Tue.	26.12.89	Birmingham City	H	D 0-0	6573
Sat.	30.12.89	Tranmere Rovers	H	W 2-0	6825
Mon.	1. 1.90	Rotherham United	A	L 2-3	
Sat.	13. 1.90	Mansfield Town	H	D 1-1	5339
Sat.	20. 1.90	Brentford	A	L 1-2	

Sat.	28. 1.90	Bolton Wanderers	H	D 1-1	7722
Sat.	10. 2.90	Preston North End	A	W 1-0	
Sun.	18. 2.90	Walsall	H	W 2-0	6226
Sat.	24. 2.90	Swansea City	A	D 0-0	
Sat.	3. 3.90	Wigan Athletic	H	W 6-1	5139
Tue.	6. 3.90	Reading	A	W 1-0	
Sun.	11. 3.90	Leyton Orient	H	D 0-0	7018
Sat.	17. 3.90	Fulham	A	W 2-1	
Wed.	21. 3.90	Bury	H	W 2-1	5552
Sat.	24. 3.90	Cardiff City	H	W 2-1	4631
Sat.	31. 3.90	Northampton Town	A	W 2-1	
Wed.	4. 4.90	Wigan Athletic	A	W 2-1	
Sat.	7. 4.90	Chester City	H	W 2-1	6589
Tue.	10. 4.90	Huddersfield Town	A	D 1-1	
Sat.	14. 4.90	Rotherham United	H	W 2-0	6794
Mon.	16. 4.90	Birmingham City	A	D 2-2	
Sat.	21. 4.90	Crewe Alexandra	H	D 1-1	7250
Mon.	23. 4.90	Tranmere Rovers	A	W 2-1	
Thurs.	26. 4.90	Notts County	A	L 1-3	
Sat.	28. 4.90	Shrewsbury Town	H	W 1-0	7903
Wed.	2. 5.90	Bristol City	H	W 3-0	9013
Sat.	5. 5.90	Blackpool	A	W 3-0	

Littlewoods League Cup

Date		Opposition	H/A	Res./Sc.	Att.
Wed.	23. 8.89	Portsmouth	H	W 1-0	4727
Tue.	29. 8.89	Portsmouth	A	L 0-2	

F.A. Cup

Date		Opposition	H/A	Res./Sc.	Att.
Sat.	18.11.89	Reading	H	D 1-1	6115
Tue.	21.11.89	Reading	A	D 1-1	
Mon.	27.11.89	Reading	H	L 0-1	6782

Leyland-Daf Cup

Date		Opposition	H/A	Res./Sc.	Att.
Tue.	7.11.89	Torquay	A	D 1-1	
Wed.	17. 1.90	Exeter City	H	W 3-0	3136
Wed.	21. 1.90	Gillingham	H	W 1-0	2724
Tue.	6. 2.90	Brentford	A	W	
Wed.	14. 3.90	Walsall	H	W 3-2	4740
Wed.	28. 3.90	Notts County	H	W 1-0	6480
Mon.	2. 4.90	Notts County	A	D 0-0	
Sun.	20. 5.90	Tranmere Rovers	Wembley	L 0-1	